RIVER
EARTH

May 23, 2000

Merry,

Thanks for all of your good work for the campus and for your friendly greetings. We wish you the very best, good health and a happy life.

R. Luce

**Other Books in the Washington State University Press
Northwest Voices Essay Series**

Louis J. Masson
Reflections: Essays on Place and Family
(1996)

Stephen J. Lyons
Landscape of the Heart: Writings on Daughters and Journeys
(1996)

Robert Schnelle
Valley Walking: Notes on the Land
(1997)

Sam Wright
Edge of Tomorrow: An Arctic Year
(1998)

RIVER EARTH

A Personal Map

JOHN C. PIERCE

WSU
PRESS

Washington State University Press
Pullman, Washington

Washington State University Press
P.O. Box 645910
Pullman, Washington 99164-5910
Phone: 800-354-7360 FAX: 509-335-8568
email: wsupress@wsu.edu
www.publications.wsu.edu/wsupress
© 1999 by the Board of Regents of Washington State University
First printing 1999

Cover illustration by Jo Hockenhull
Library of Congress Cataloging-in-Publication Data

Pierce, John C., 1943–
    River earth : a personal map / John C. Pierce : illustrations by
Jo Hockenhull.
        p.   cm. — (Northwest voices essay series)
    ISBN 0-87422-176-5. — ISBN 0-87422-177-3 (pbk.)
    1. Pierce, John C., 1943 -   . 2. Northwest, Pacific—Biography.
3. Jeru Creek Region (Idaho)—Biography. 4. Rivers—Northwest,
Pacific—Anecdotes. 5. Fly fishing—Northwest, Pacific—Anecdotes.
I. Title. II. Series.
CT275.P637A3   1999
799.1'24—dc21   99-17125
                                                          CIP

Contents

"Tales From Jeru Creek," Jo Hockenhull, 1999

Preface

AFLY FISHING FRIEND who read an earlier version of *River Earth* asked that I make clear right at the start that these essays are not about fly fishing, even though there is some fly fishing in them. I think there was some disappointment in his request, hoping, as he was, to obtain some little insight from a successful trek on a stream someplace. Although that friend kept reading, others searching for trout laden secrets about river and stream will need to look elsewhere.

I started writing these essays about four years ago. It was a very different kind of enterprise than that to which I had been accustomed. I am a social scientist who relies on empirical data to tell me about the world of politics. This venture, though, was much more a journey to find out about myself than about the world. My writing began as I entered my fifties. My two sons had left home and increasingly stretched our very tight bands, and I hunted for some way to accommodate and understand the gaps they left in my life. My writing continued on through the physical decline and death of my mother, a silent but courageous "first wave feminist," a portion of whose life appears in several of these stories. This also has been a time when I have made some crucial choices about the last decade or so of my personal and professional life, leaving a home and a workplace of nearly twenty-five years for new challenges a thousand miles away. And, new friends and old have asked me pointed questions about who I am (or maybe, who do I think I am?) and why I am doing the things I am. I did not often have the answers.

I read some of the early stories to a few friends, people I thought would treat me with both the care and the honesty the best of that relationship demands. They encouraged me to keep writing. They also said I should put these pieces in a form that would be accessible at least to my family, and perhaps to others through a more public printing. So, I continued to write, trying never to stray from the personal source of the essays.

As I got through a very early draft I took the manuscript to Keith Petersen at WSU Press. I knew Keith would give me an honest reading about if and where I might publish the manuscript, since he had rejected several of my more scholarly submissions to the Press. Keith said he thought WSU Press might be interested in the collection if I were willing to make a number of changes. Over the subsequent several years Keith has guided me with frank and valuable advice about what to expand, what to eliminate, and what to change. There is a lot here that was not included when he first looked at my work, and a lot of what was there no longer can be found. To the degree those changes enhance the book, he deserves the credit.

Susan Wyche read the entire manuscript several times. She worked on my grammar and on my style, and asked me many a tough question. She was willing to enter into the book from the unique perspective of both honest friend and honest critic. Her encouragement to keep writing was crucial to the completion of the manuscript. Pat McManus read an early version of the book and gave me helpful comments. Dr. Harold Simonson, my college English teacher, responded to a blind inquiry on my part, and thirty years after I was undistinguished in his class, consented to read one of the intermediate versions of the manuscript. His advice was telling, and crucial to the shape of the current essays. Julia Davis, Mary Wack, Marilyn Ihinger-Tallman, Al Kitchel, Rick Pride, Jim Thurber, John Donnelly, David Spencer, Sue McCleod, Missye Bonds, Leigh Stowell, Terry Flynn, Deborah Haynes, Jim White, Sandy Kraemer, Alex Kuo, and others I have neglected to mention all read, or listened to me read, or talk about, all or part of *River Earth*. Leigh and Marilyn Stowell, our wonderful friends, and their daughters Erica and Stephanie, gave me an added gift when they sat huddled under a canvas tarp in a cold rain high above 10,000 feet on the continental divide in Wyoming while I tried out some of the chapters found here. And Press Stephens, the art historian outfitter who guided us on that Absoraka Mountain adventure, gave me unintentional insight into how to write about my son Forrest. Anne Smith worked hard on making the first version of *River Earth* legible and consistent in format and frame, and reading it while she did so she gave me unintentional but much needed encouragement to go on. And my compassionate, beautiful, and tolerant wife Ardith drove across Washington state many times while I insisted on reading chapters to her from the passenger side of the front seat, for some reason not allowing me to read and drive at the same time. Nick and Katherine Lovrich, Hal and Joan Dengerink, Herb and Jann Hill—our dear friends and cabin neighbors on Jeru Creek—provided the human leavening for *River Earth*, as well as the inspiration for many stories not included here.

In the final analysis, though, for better and for worse, these essays are simply an outgrowth of who I am, and the fact that moving water forces me to reflect on both. As I re-read the essays, I find that I too have changed in the time since they first were authored. And writing about it all has changed how I look at myself, where I have been, and perhaps shifted where I am going.

The title of the book, *River Earth*, is shamelessly derived from William Least Heat-Moon's *PrairyErth*, which I once reviewed. "River Earth" obviously makes little sense from a literal perspective. But, after writing the title essay, which took shape sometime in the middle of the book's evolution, I was struck by two things. First, I saw the tension between the seemingly fixed and unmoving nature of the earth on the one hand, and the ever-moving life-like character of the river on the other hand; that juxtaposition seemed obvious as a source of personal reflection. But second, it seemed to me that the river itself has its own internal mix of stability and change; the river provides a focal point for viewing a life constructed from the mix of the internal motion of the river itself and the stable reference it provides for those around it. In fact, the seeming paradox of the title reflects the ambivalence and uncertainty I felt as I tried to untangle my own feelings about the subjects of the essays, and both the people and the places in them.

I dedicate this book to my family—Ardith, Forrest, and Lamar—about whom I have written much in these pages, and to Jaci and Amanda, the two wonderful, spirited, beautiful daughters-in-law who have merged with us and welcomed me into their lives. I must ask my family and friends to have empathy for the transgressions of their privacy. They know I love them deeply. I am blessed by the love that they return without reservation, even as they know the man reflected in these pages.

John C. Pierce
Colorado Springs, Colorado
February 1999

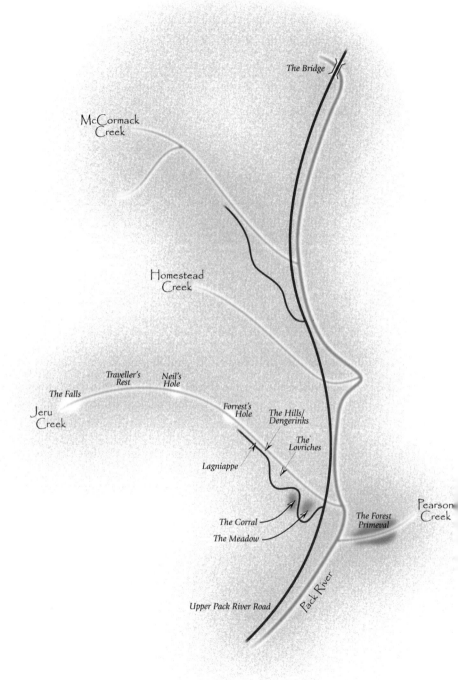

The Bridge

McCormack
Creek

Homestead
Creek

Traveller's
Rest

Neil's
Hole

The Falls

Forrest's
Hole

Jeru
Creek

The Hills/
Dengerinks

The
Lovriches

Lagniappe

Pearson
Creek

The Corral

The Forest
Primeval

The Meadow

Pack River

Upper Pack River Road

1
Riverfishing

"WHY DO YOU LOVE RIVERS SO?" she asked. Until that seemingly simple query I had thought little about why moving waters mean so much to me. In reflection, though, I think there is an answer, lodged deep in the remnants of my childhood memory. In the logging and farming community where I was raised, fishing a river marked a pivotal entry into manhood. In my adolescent world, going "riverfishing" would mean that I had grown up. No longer could I be shunted to the children's table at the family Thanksgiving dinner. No more would I be forced to share a bedroom with my grandmother when she came to visit. Most of all, though, to fish a river would be irrefutable evidence in my father's eyes that I had become strong enough to protect my own life in the hidden currents of nature. The time would have come when I no longer would be in need of my father's uncompromising approval.

Freedom from my father's emotional rein was not an easy grace to gain. He surely cared for us deeply, but the obvious anguish of the dustbowl-thwarted aspirations of his youth, coupled with his dark periods of brooding silence and anger, left his children balanced between fear and love. No violence ever emerged from his times of pain, but we searched for those rare moments when we might meet the high standards he set for us. For me, going riverfishing with my father would mean that I had arrived at that favored station.

At least in the dreams of my early youth, then, the chance to go riverfishing with my father was to be one of the most significant events of my life. As I grew up, I waited with impatient hope for the time when my father could convince both himself and my mother that it would be safe to take me with him on the opening day of fishing on the lowland streams of western Washington.

But riverfishing with my father was a turning point in my life that never happened. And the importance of never riverfishing with my father seems clear to me now, even from the shadowy perspective of more than four decades and the graying filter of the adult looking back in time. I know now that not going riverfishing with my father has led to my unending fascination with rivers, and with the streams and creeks that mimic them.

Long before I crept up on the time when I could hope to go riverfishing with my father, I had been more casually initiated into the sedentary experience of "lakefishing." That exercise on the local ponds posed little mystery and no excitement for me. We did wonder whether we would be able to maneuver our way through the long lines of cars containing the lake fisherman in a hurry to get to recently stocked Lawrence Lake. I recall clearly the sleek and slippery evidence when my father and uncles would come home from the lake and spread out their catch on newspapers on the lawn. But even the prospect of catching twenty healthy hatchery-grown trout with worms, cured salmon eggs, and marshmallows, or corn, dipped over the side of an anchored rowboat, never approached the high hopes rising from the possibility of going riverfishing.

My father died of a heart attack when he was only forty-three and I was but thirteen. It was not even deep enough into that summer of 1957 for there to have been a father-led riverfishing reprieve from a lifelong sentence. Still, my fading, reconstructed memory tells me that if not that summer, for sure the following one, my father would have taken me riverfishing, and we could have shared the ritual passage for which I still wait.

The summer before my father's death I had been given a peek into the coming riverfishing ceremony while on one of the charter salmon fishing boats at the Pacific Ocean village of Westport. We had driven the several hours to the coast with a group of my father's male friends to join in the local Lion's Club collective trip (the "Salmon Derby"). While I surely felt grown up and manly to be included on the long trip, the memory of that experience recalls no great thrill. On my rented rod we did catch the biggest salmon of the Lion's Club derby, and a picture of my father and me proudly standing on the pier appeared in the *Nisqually Valley News* the next week.

This photo appeared in the *Nisqually Valley News* on August 23, 1956, with the following caption: Shirley Pierce, shown on the right with his son, John, was crowned King of Yelm Lions Club fishermen following the club's outing last Sunday at Westport. Pierce, shown holding his pride and joy, was awarded a complete salt water fishing outfit for his prowess with the pole.

The problem with the salmon derby at Westport was that between rapid trips to the side of the vessel, I spent almost the entire voyage in the hold of the charter boat. I was in agony at the nausea that perhaps signified to father my apparent unreadyness to take on the truly mature aspects of the adult male's rituals, including riverfishing. That rocking, swell-carried boat trip marked my first venture into a motion sickness syndrome that still haunts me as an adult, surfacing in airplanes, on merry-go-rounds, Ferris

Wheels, roller coasters, and on playground swings. At some level, that vomitous ocean ride may explain why to this day I like to fish with my feet on something solid, like the rocks of a river.

What makes this failed passage to the river with my father more painful to me is that in my memory, at least, we almost went riverfishing. Late in the spring before my father died, the beginning of the stream and river fishing season was on the horizon. I had been watching my father closely, trying to sense the signals that would suggest that I might soon be his companion on the river. I knew that even the most evenhanded pleading I could muster would only put off longer the time when I would go riverfishing. The invitation to accompany my father fishing would come only when the time was right, and only by his reckoning and not mine. Any hint of whining would surely be further evidence of my unreadyness.

I lay in bed the night before the start of the riverfishing season, listening to the animated discussion in the living room. My father and my mother were engaged in heated words over whether I could go riverfishing the next morning, opening day. They talked loudly and stridently as my father laid out his gear—an old bamboo rod that, until my mother's death some forty years later, I still searched for in the attic whenever I returned to her home; a handmade tin stripping basket that was held precariously around my father's waist; a leather zippered and tooled wallet that harbored an assortment of dry and wet flies; and a woven wicker creel.

That creel now serves as the ballast for an indoor mobile of two, three-foot long, translucent salmon sculptures that swim in the windows of the garden room of our home. The hand-tooled wallet now hangs on the wall above my desk, containing both the ancient flies of my father and my own early amateurish attempts to match north Idaho insects. The stripping basket also now rests on my study wall, the object of a quiz I give to every modern flyfisher who comes to visit. "What do you think that thing is?" I ask.

While the guesses range from a breastplate to bait skimmer, none of the guests can produce the right answer. These accoutrements of my father's riverfishing ventures remain the sole material legacy of the trip that never happened.

Even so, the night before my father's scheduled solitary trip to the river, I held guarded aspirations that the morning might bring a reprieve from another Sunday of waiting for him to return home with the confirmation of his own abilities on the river. I prayed that father would win the argument, that mother would change her mind or give in and release me to the river with him. That journey was not to be.

That memory of the Sunday morning at home is full of regret. It is not simply that I never had a chance to go riverfishing with my father. Rather, if my parents had only talked a little more, that symbolic crossing into adulthood might yet have happened. My father came home from the river, and on the kitchen counter he laid out a half dozen small native cutthroat for us to admire. While I was quite impressed with the fruits of his fishing, my mother said with some bemusement, "You caught those in the Nisqually?"

The Nisqually is the local glacial river known for its erratic water levels because of an upstream dam, and for its deep hidden holes, lying in wait at the bottom of both pools and riffles. The Nisqually also holds some rather large trout, including summer run steelhead and sea-run cutthroat. My father replied, "No those came from the Deschutes." The Deschutes of Washington, unlike the famed namesake of eastern Oregon, is a small, meandering stream of lazy summertime dreams. The Deschutes wanders through hay fields and enters and retreats from the remnant fir forests of the Cascade foothills, but rarely threatens with the same fierceness as the Nisqually.

Mother's response sits painfully with me still. "Oh, I thought you were going fishing in the Nisqually. That's why I didn't want

John to go with you. If I had known it was the Deschutes, he could have gone. It is fine with me if he goes the next time."

The "next time" disappeared forever that summer, along with my father's life. So, at the bottom of some riffle of my own internal river, there remains a lingering pain from the loss of that first riverfishing trip, the one that never happened. My longed-for passageway into adulthood in my father's company was blocked by both the dearth of communication and the shock of his unexpected death. In some ways, my love for rivers must reflect a searching for that passage still. My love for rivers is an attempt to find, as son, a voiceless channel to that filial knitting that comes from sharing space in a stream.

Now I am a father and I still embrace the emotion of riverfishing. The film *A River Runs Through It* spawned a voguish interest in flyfishing. Not only the beauty of the river scenes and the incomparable backcasts in the sunset, but the dynamics of a strong father and two equally strong sons struck a special chord in our family. The passage into manhood, and the struggles for independence and for individuality that were cast so starkly in the movie, also have been present in my own family. The rivers— whatever streams or creeks they happen to be—have joined me to my two sons in a way I had hoped they would link me with my father. The rupture of my future with him has led me to the hope that such a time will not be lost in the third generation of our riverfishing family.

It probably has been selfish, my trying to capture what had not been possible in my own life by the early introduction of my sons to riverfishing. But I cannot escape the truth that creek and riverfishing have been an inseparable component of the bonds of the male triangle in our family, growing tighter and tighter since the time my sons could walk on their own. My sons and I often fish in pairs, but the true synergy and the tussles and struggles of our personalities come when we all three fish together—I, the

John, Lamar, and Forrest

father, with the need for things to be right, not only in the fishing, but also among us; Forrest, the older of the sons, the tall blond who played basketball, loves to create music, and hates to kill a fish; Lamar, the younger of the siblings, tall, inquisitive, who also played both music and basketball but whose early goal in life was to prove he was better than his father and his brother, and who now knows that in his own space he has succeeded, and that where he has not it makes no difference.

In riverfishing, though, the three of us have now found a place where there is no need to best each other—where there is little compulsion to prove that I am still the father and the fisher; where Forrest has forsaken the unnecessary mission to prove that he is a man, and better than his father; and, where Lamar no longer tries to prove that he always is better than his brother, who is better than his father.

In riverfishing, my sons and I find wonder in where we are, and in the closeness that knits us so tightly. Together, we walk the river, often in the pretense of fishing, but really searching for the best huckleberries. Or we find the cavern holding the biggest, deepest pool for skinny-dipping. And we look for the yellow shaft of light, angled obliquely through the cedar and the larch into the bronzed river bottom.

Forrest and Lamar go off by themselves sometimes, usually to the very high lakes where I only reluctantly wander these days. I miss those trips. Sometimes I go out on the river alone because one of them is in Aspen or Indiana doing music, and the other is in Olympia or Berkeley doing economics. It is then that I have this deep ache in me that I feel elsewhere only when I go into the sanctuary of a church. I saw my own father at church only once—in the shadows of the back row during my Palm Sunday baptism three months before he died. And it was in church where every Sunday my two sons sat with me for years while their mother sang in the choir.

I have not quite understood that ache when I am on the river, or in the church, until now, and even now only vaguely. I know now though that it is a bittersweet ache of love, a love lost in my memory of my father who died so young before we could go riverfishing. It is a love both of then and of now that was built and rebuilt on the creeks and streams. It is an ache of love that is stretched like the river itself in the absence of my sons now in their own lives and whose shared affection peaks on the river. It is of a love that I pray will not again be lost when their father is gone.

I must confess how hard it is for me to write about this emotional attachment to rivers in anything more than clichés and triteness. In my life the cliché is born of the redundant truth, and the trite is spawned by the commonplace joy. I collect and read books about rivers, especially when the water and the person seem to speak to each other in a language only faintly heard by others. *A River Runs Through It*, *The River Why*, *The Habit of Rivers*, and the rest of this growing genre all have their own mystique, their own lyric, their own touch of self-congratulatory wonder.

How can my answer to the question of why I love rivers so be any clearer, any better, any more insightful than those? Perhaps the answer is only in the personal nature of the response that allows it to be more than just another testimony to the marvels of moving water and the creatures that inhabit it. Even so, the self-centered caste of personal reflections on my love of rivers may isolate those thoughts from the care and ken of others. So, I try to find that elusive intersection of my own emotion and another's understanding.

In a different sense, then, distanced from family memories, it is the intrinsic paradox of the river that has seduced me. It is that juxtaposition of movement and mass that reminds me of my love for rivers. It is movement that makes the river, defines its body, gives it character and personality. Rivers emerge in my emotions because they move, because they change, because they reproduce themselves in a kind of eternal spring.

Strangely, though, the movement of the river is less clear to me from within it than from without. Once in the river, the enveloping strain of the unknown current provides a constant force against which I can lean and find stability. Only in retrospect does that stability from the constant movement of the river provide me with any metaphor for my life. Reflecting on why moving water is a source of solace and why it provides me reassurance does take me back to where I began. But even with no memories of river-fishing with my father, and in the increasing absence of my own sons, my love of rivers continues to search me out and forces me to consider both the pain and the pleasure of the personal past.

2

River Earth

AN I REALLY COME TO KNOW who I am through reflection on my own experience? And in that self-centered introspection, what provides the personal point of reference, that external marker of my individual history? What gives shape and structure both to what I come to know and to what I project? How can I extrapolate both forward and backward to reasonable explanations for the person I am and for what arc I will travel on my own particular trajectory?

So, where am I going? Several years ago I was asked to recommend a book to incoming freshmen at Washington State University. Along with reviews by some other faculty and some famous graduates the result was printed in a small publication and sent to the future students. Each of us picked a different work on which to focus. *PrairyErth*, the book I reviewed, has remained with me as have few others. That book seems to have special relevance for me as I think and write about the sources in and of my life. *PrairyErth* strangely continues to come forward as I try to update who I am from my filtering of what in fact comes and goes, both before and after now, and from where those real and imaginary travels took place.

William Least Heat-Moon, in *PrairyErth*, conducted what English literature professors might call a "close reading" of Chase County, Kansas. Chase County is a far distance from the Thurston County, Washington, of my own childhood. On the other hand, it is not so far from the southern Nebraska, Platte River-bordering grassland from which my parents emigrated in the dustbowl depression days of the late 1930s. Chase County contains the Flint Hills, "the last remaining grand expanse of tallgrass prairie in the United States."

That tallgrass prairie can seem a largely barren landscape, but the Flint Hills are clearly dotted with the remnants of both the native peoples and the more recent European settlers. Brush and tree-laden creek and river bottoms, small towns, isolated and forgotten homesteads, old cemeteries, abandoned tracks, and (most importantly) people of all kinds—these provide the fertile surface from which *PrairyErth* is born. Beneath that surface is a splendid web of interwoven explorations of local natural and human history, personalities, geography, geology, anthropology, economics, wildlife, environment, and politics. That web provides a context within which to understand what now is there, why it and its people are shaped the way they are. And the writing of Least Heat-Moon serves as a model for an understanding of other places and other people.

Heat-Moon's travels were much more systematic than any of my own wanderings; he divided Chase County in quadrangles, and then physically and metaphorically entered each quadrangle to its center point. He walked the land and he probed the people. He set foot, and bottom, in the local tavern to talk with the old-timers. He languished on the hilltop in the middle of the night. And he spent hours asking and listening—to the people, to the land, and to their conversations with each other. Heat-Moon also moved backwards in history, laterally in topography, and forward in social prophecy as he knit together all of the disparate strands of life and land in the Flint Hills.

As I read *PrairyErth* I was inevitably drawn to reflect on my own understanding of where I had spent much of my early life. My childhood home was a mountain range and the Columbia Basin away from where I lived for more than twenty years in the Palouse country of eastern Washington, and a thousand miles from the mountain shadows of the Colorado Front Range where we now find root. Yelm, Washington, is where I grew up, and who I now am cannot escape the life I had there. Yelm was where I first learned to fish rivers, to wade creeks and streams, to walk up and down the small main street and visit with the local businessmen who had befriended me. Those community leaders engaged in a kind of collective paternal oversight of me after my father died the summer just before I entered high school. In retrospect, I guess I was a youthful anthropologist. I was able to talk with the local newspaper editor, the jeweler, the barber, the hardware store owner, the guy who ran the dry goods part of the local department/grocery store, the owner of D and H Garage, and the old man who showed up one day during the depression and for decades swept the streets of the town and slept in a little shack just down the road from our house. I know that the time I spent walking Yelm Avenue has left me unable to ignore the imperative of civic life, a belief in the collective responsibility we have to make our places better.

Unlike William Least Heat-Moon, though, who came to Flint Hills for a while, did his close observation, and left, my reflections about Yelm stem from the fact that I was raised there. I grew up in the shadows of the "Bald Hills" (called that because of their barrenness after the first sweep of clearcutting through the forested foothills of western Washington), and my time there is an inseparable part of the life I want to describe. Each type of experience—the intensive short-term study by Heat-Moon or the intensive involvement of my own social education in a hometown—provides a unique entry into the knowledge of a special place, of a "prairyerth" or (in a clear and shameless extension) a "river earth," and a unique entry into the labyrinth of the shadowed ignorance of my own life.

Until I read *PrairyErth* I thought I knew Yelm, Thurston County, Washington. And in some ways I suppose I did know Yelm, a community whose name is said to derive from "shelm," the native term for the shimmering summer heat waves rising from the area's own prairie grass. Most of us do know our hometown in a way that an "outsider" like William Least Heat-Moon cannot possibly hope to approach. Yet, the lesson—and the fascination—of a *PrairyErth* is that it shows how our insight into our own hometown, and thus into ourselves, is also inadequate. Heat-Moon shows us how much there is to know, how little we grasp, and how diverse and demanding is the task to close the gap between the two.

Trying to draw close that gulf between what is hidden in the past and what can be apprehended now, or for that matter, what can be portended for the future, is even more difficult when tracking through the prairie of one's memory. That uncertain travel back through my own time to my own origin, as I try to reconstruct the jigsaw puzzle of my past, brings another truth. The passage of time produces a bittersweet tug. I understand my own hometown because I was an integral part of it for some time. But the town surely has changed and so have I. So my memories are shadowed by the growing ignorance that stems from becoming the outsider into which I have inevitably developed.

The defining construction of my life in and exit from Yelm, and my memory-based re-entry into the Yelm prairie (by the way, this is not an artificial device linking prairie to prairyerth; the local summer celebration is called "prairie days" and Yelm is self-labeled as the "pride of the prairie"), always has been the creeks and the rivers. For many a young man, the local rivers provided the passage into manhood. Too, the rivers and streams always defined and illuminated other portions of my life in Yelm. It was to the rivers that I would retreat alone to try to redress the solitude and the pain of teenage life, whether generated from the absence of close friends in a small town where few if any shared my rather idiosyncratic mixture of love for academics, aesthetics, athletics, and the outdoors, or from the continuing search for some stability and constancy in a world that had so recently been shaken by my father's death.

But hanging over the prairie, and all of the rivers, and all of our lives, was the even more constant presence of "The

Mountain." Standing as a fixed counterpoint to the movement of the rivers, Mt. Rainier is a mystical presence of mythological proportions. My bedroom window looked straight to the east, where, on the rare cloudless morning, the sun would rise directly behind Mt. Rainier, casting an aurora of religious implications around the massive, fourteen thousand foot, still-active volcano. I cannot think of that home without thinking of the mountain.

All of us who grew up on the Yelm prairie oriented our lives by the mountain. The first conscious observation in the morning was whether the "mountain is out," imputing a kind of anthropomorphic volition to the huge mass dominating the horizon. We oriented ourselves geographically by the mountain, driving toward it, or away from it. My mother predicted the weather by the cloud formations settled in the empty cone of the former top of the volcano. The mountain is said to have been the home of a deity for the native peoples, and for some a forbidden sanctuary onto which one stepped with only great risk.

The mountain, though, is more than an omnipresence, and more than a home for a god. The mountain also is the source, the wellspring of some of the lowland rivers that sustained cultures, and fisheries, and communication, and provided so much of the richness of my own life there. The Nisqually travels through Yelm Prairie, which is midway between the river's icy birth and its saltwater demise. The river ekes slowly out of one of the great glaciers on the flank of the mountain (the Nisqually glacier) and is augmented by the heavy rains of the western Cascade watershed. Often, the tumbling river, even as it nears the bottom portions of its route, carries with it much of the silt from the glacier-encrusted mountain that feeds it from the start. The sometimes milky white river water is a constant reminder of the ice age origin of the entire area, ground down by the inexorable force of an oncoming wall of rock and cold, and the boulder strewn prairie floor remains where the receding glacier left behind its rounded moraine.

The often-clouded color of the Nisqually River also carries with it some of the same mystery and fear as that shrouding its mountain mother. The Nisqually River has claimed its share of lives even within my memory. Dammed for power, the river is subject to rapid increases in its depth, stranding both waders and boaters on the rocks that remain in midstream, or sucking them down into hidden holes on the bottom. I remember in particular the death of the father of a family in town, who had tried to rescue an incautious visitor, and who himself then became a victim of the river. The legacy of the river taking from the town a good person always seemed to imply both the ever present danger of the opaque, unknown stream, and the frequent futility of defying that danger in the hope of doing the right thing.

Perhaps the real meaning of river earth is the connection to the native peoples from which the Nisqually takes its name. The Nisqually Reservation sits astride a state highway, with the reservation boundaries almost bordering the town of Yelm. Passage from Yelm to Olympia, the state capital, requires driving on that highway through the reservation. The Nisqually is not a very big reservation, and in a kind of historic irony itself is neighbored by the Fort Lewis Military Reservation. Olympia is about fifteen miles from Yelm, and long before McDonald's came to town, as high school students we drove to Olympia or its suburbs for a hamburger and a milkshake, always passing through both reservations at night, down a long tunnel of fog-dripping fir trees. More than once we were stopped late at night by military people on some kind of war game as they hunted for the enemy in the car, although I suspect what they really wanted to inspect were the young women who accompanied us. While the Nisqually Reservation did not ride heavy on our consciousness, it was always present like a faint shadow on an overcast day. My sisters and I shared school with students from the reservation, and my mother taught them in the early grades. In my older sister's high school years in the early 1950s, several athletes of extraordinary talent competed for the Yelm "Tornadoes." And I was told—whether true or not, I do not know—that the young Nisqually girl who graduated in the mid-1960s with my younger sister was the first female from the reservation to complete Yelm High School. Later on, an extraordinarily talented young basketball player was killed in an automobile accident. But there are several other memories that strike more deeply at the awkward relationship of past and future, and native and newcomer.

The Nisqually River falls into the lower part of Puget Sound, through a rich delta that now is a wildlife refuge. The river has been home to many fish—steelhead, salmon, native and sea-run cutthroat and rainbow, and even the sucker-mouthed whitefish. Not surprisingly, fishing was central both to the life and to the culture of the local indigenous people. The huge lowland cedar and fir provided the dugout canoes from which the native fishermen stretched their nets across the river. I do not really know when the Nisqually fishermen stopped using dugout canoes, but I have this misty image in my own memory of seeing the dugout canoes powered by gasoline engines and the men stretching salmon nets across the river, and my own wondering about the juxtaposition of the ancient craft and the modern motor.

Native fishing rights on the Nisqually were of importance not just for the people on this particular reservation. One incident resulting from a native/state showdown over fishing rights on the river became a signal event in the development of native claims, and in the public militancy of the native peoples as they tried to ensure treaty rights. In the 1960s at Frank's Landing there were a series of confrontations between state officials and native fishermen; those incidents catalyzed and polarized political forces around the relative claims of native and non-native peoples, passing eventually into landmark judicial cases, such as the Boldt decision legally dividing access to the resource between whites and nonwhites.

My mother, as a first grade teacher, instructed a number of the young children from the reservation. She had a special combination of affection and expectation, an early version of tough love, that endeared her to the children and to their parents. My mother always seemed to have a special position in the hearts of the reservation mothers. For years she was invited to church, to weddings, to funerals on the reservation, frequently being the only non-tribal person present. She was present at Indian Shaker services in the church (not to be confused with the New England Shaker Church). And long after her retirement every once in a while a beat-up old car would pull into the driveway in front of her ancient white farm house. One of the Nisqually men would get out, go around and open the trunk, and bring out a fresh salmon or steelhead, sometimes as a gift, sometimes for sale.

One of the starkest memories of my youth of this river earth was driving to Olympia through the reservation and seeing the enormous power transmission lines that striated the long narrow forest clearing that paralleled the highway. Underneath those testaments to modernity were the homes of the reservation. At that time, many of those homes were without electricity, running water, and the other accoutrements of progress. I failed then to process the irony of that power grid, locked in the sky, high over the people whose life and culture grew out of the flowing water that produced the power but who themselves were kept apart from it. It was not until the Great Society programs of the War on Poverty that the contrast between progress and past somehow reached the consciousness of someone in power.

Three decades later, down that same highway to Olympia, through the same shrouded funnel of firs, not only are there many reservation homes obviously with electricity and the positive and negative attributes of contemporary life, but also there is a bingo hall. There is something unsettling to me about the transition from the dugout canoe to the bingo hall, with power—economic, electric, and political—acquired along the way.

Not too long ago, driving through the reservation, I looked away from the bingo parlor side of the road, down into the river area where the traditional homes had stood, and where the traditional lives had been led. Perhaps in another flash of accidental irony, I saw the signs that marked the entry to the lanes leading to the river. At each entrance to the old life, and directed away from the bingo hall, was a black-on-yellow rectangle that said "Dead End."

The stream of progress, the bingo hall, the flow of electric power, the channel of cars through the night—they all seem to have replaced the river. The river is still there, of course, and there is some rebirth of native religion and culture along its banks, but its centrality to the life there now seems more symbolic, albeit no less real. The native peoples themselves recognize that change and that sense of loss, and there often surface stories of attempts to recapture the spiritual and cultural links to the land and the river. The secret societies and the sun ceremony and the ritualistic taking of the fish all point to a fundamental need to identify with and affirm the connection between who one is and river earth.

River earth helps me understand that there is something that unites river and earth when they both play the same nurturing role for the people who live on or near them. The river may be the mother for the soul. It enriches, it shelters, it cradles, it provides a resting place for my unease. Even when it is not possible to place myself very comfortably in the going and the coming of family or community or geography, the river can give me solace. It provides a point of reference, an assurance that while the river remains, it also is a source of change. The floods recede, just as surely as they come.

Winter of 1996 brought re-affirmation of river earth, and of the lessons I learned growing up there, lessons about the interconnectedness of life, death, change, and the physical and emotional power of nature. The Nisqually River flooded and took a terrible human and environmental toll, some say because of the deliberate release of water from a power-generating dam upstream. My mother died in February of that year also. She died during those floods. For a while the flood water impeded access to her home for returning family, at least via the time-honored route through the Nisqually Reservation.

Along with much of the old community, several Nisqually women came to my mother's memorial service in our church, returning the ritual acknowledgment of passing she had given to them so many times. One of the eulogies to my mother drew parallels between her pioneer independence and compassion and the need for similar qualities in the collective response to flood-induced hardships. As I sat there in the church, a melancholy mix of joy and sadness seemed seated in me, rooted in the realization of the release by my mother's physical passage. But that nesting of emotion emerges also in the webbing of a social fabric that re-knits itself in death's signal moment. I know now that the message of who I am is provided by the intermingling of the unending cycles of both floods and family in river earth.

3
Fly Fishing Alone

AESTHETICALLY, I SUPPOSE I AM not a very good fly fisher. To be sure, I have watched and read *A River Runs Through It* and I have seen lots of outdoor videos on television. *Gray's Sporting Journal, Outdoor Life, Field and Stream*, and several hundred fishing books crowd my shelves. Nonetheless, the connection between what I do and what the experts claim to do seems fuzzy at best. Regularly, I must remind myself that the purpose is not to fish for art, but to fish for fish, and that much of the true wonder of fly fishing emerges from the loneliness I find in the act, not in the elegance contained in the art of it. Indeed, fly fishing leads my thoughts far from the stream, and the more alone I am the more distant my mind travels.

That I am an artless fly fisher does not have to mean that I fail to catch fish using a fly rod with dry, wet, or streamer imitations of insects. In fact, every summer in front of credible witnesses I am able to deceive hundreds of beautiful cutthroat and rainbow trout in the mountain streams near our north Idaho cabin. On occasion, it seems, the fish and I just seem to agree that the moment is right for the fly.

To be honest, though, I have rarely tried to match the hatch, or to fish with the nearly invisible imitations of midges; nor have I crouched in streamside shadows, anticipating the annual Mayfly emergence. In fact, I am not sure that I would recognize a Mayfly if it flew up in my face. It also is true that unlike the masters of the craft, I rarely use a hook smaller than a number 12, and usually it is a size 10. Number 10 is the size I started out fly fishing with because that was what I used for eggs and worms when going after the hatchery trout briefly residing in the streams of western Washington. I see no reason why the little trout of northern Idaho would want anything smaller.

I will admit that the relatively massive size of the flies I use—in comparison to the naturals and to the trout I catch—is occasionally the subject of some bemusement and not too little condescension among the experts who sometimes accompany me. These are not my experts, I want it known, but those attached to my relatives and friends. I have no experts of my own. These experts do catch fish too, and in a fashion much prettier than the way I do it.

The other reason I continue to use a size 10 hook is that these days I am having trouble getting the leader through the eye of something even that big. As they say, art is in the eye of the beholder, and age clearly constrains the art of fishing with very small hooks. But to be honest, the art never was there anyway.

When I fish, I have only three or four patterns that I use with any regularity. What fly I use depends on the time of the summer (Renegades and Yellow Humpies most of the summer, but ants and black flies later on), what I've got in my fly tin because my friend in Corvallis tied them, what the weekly report in the paper claims, and what the guy at the Pastime Cafe in Sandpoint, Idaho, has to sell. For a while I tied my own flies, but even when following the directions of the manual, the columnist in the local newspaper, or my neighbor, my products bore little resemblance either to the living model or to the full color picture in front of me. But, they were my flies.

The first flies I tied were an attempt to match the successful pattern I used in northern Idaho when I started fishing the streams of the Selkirk Mountains. In the 1970s, some twenty years after my father's death, I was rummaging around in my mother's attic and found my father's old leather fly pouch. I brought the pouch to our cabin and used some of the wet and dry flies it contained, most of which had rusted hooks and torn hackles. One of the flies was particularly successful and I failed to find anything resembling it in any of the books, or in the fly shops. So, I tried to create a reasonable facsimile. I never did, and the clumsy effort produced many biologically unreasonable but fairly parsimonious models of the insect world.

Strangely, though, with the ugly flies and the few reliable patterns purchased downtown, I caught fish, sometimes several hundred in a day—again with reliable witnesses—out of a small mountain river. Now, these fish rarely exceed ten or eleven inches in length, although I once caught a twenty-three-inch spawning cutthroat (but to be honest, not on a fly, although I once had one that big hooked on a little dry fly, but not hooked for long). The fish are beautiful, colorful, brazen, and full of fight. The best part is brazen, which probably is why my unaesthetic approach to the sport is successful. And, the fish are found in, and returned to, some of the most spectacular high mountain streams imaginable. We (usually my two sons and I) climb steep canyons, scale down slides, crawl through brush, and fish literally within the shadows of great granite domes. The water is so clear that we never know how deep the pool goes, but we do see the strikes as the bright native trout ascend from the bottom to whatever level the dry fly reaches.

There are lots of lakes in the mountains ringing the river valley. These lakes feed the creeks, the streams, and the river that we invade. But, as beautiful as the lakes appear, I have never fly fished any of them, and I have little desire to do so. For some reason the mountain lakes just fail to mesh with my psyche. Oh, I think it is acceptable to describe them as jewels in the crowns of the mountains, or whatever. But lakes don't really do anything, at least not at any tempo with which I can stay in tune. They just sit there, like the curated relics of an ancient geology. Frankly, mountain lakes are boring. They also are difficult to fish, especially if one is a lousy wielder of the flyrod. So, I am thankful for the mountain lakes mainly because they are the source of the streams I ply.

Once with my friend Reid Miller I set out to fish one of those high lakes. It was alleged to be at the end of a very long and steep walk up abandoned logging roads. About two-thirds of the way up we stopped to rest on a great outlook. We then peered back down into the valley. There, what seemed like several thousand feet below us, was a set of pearl-like pools in a heretofore hidden stretch of a sinewy creek. I could not resist. We turned and started back down the logging road, and discovered another wonderful stretch of lousy fly fishing.

Another reason I do not fish mountain lakes is that I don't like to fish anything that is too big, or too deep, for me to become a part. And, that goes for rivers as well. I have to be able to become part of the water's flow, to wade down the middle, to cross at will, to fall in and not worry about climbing out. I think that it is that capacity to become part of the stream that enables me to gain so much emotionally from being out there by myself.

I think I wore wading boots once, and found them too cumbersome to let me go with ease into the mountain runs and pools. Though I do not wade through every pool or trudge up the middle of every riffle, I have to be able to do so if it feels right. As a youth, I started out fishing with just a tee shirt, cut-offs, and tennis shoes. Now I protect myself a little more—I usually wear socks. The Devil's Club and the nettles that line the stream banks are less tolerable than they were twenty or thirty years ago. And the pain from falling off the logs and landing in the rocks just under the water seems to be more intense and to last a little longer than before. So, sometimes I wear long pants and a long shirt, and soon I will graduate into felt-soled wading shoes. But they do make me feel less like a fish and more like a fly fisherman—an evolution that rests uneasily on my conscience.

I must confess that the way I go fly fishing scares my wife. Ardith has seen me run the river rocks, jumping at top speed as I race to the next promising spot. But that was when we were newlyweds. Actually, on our honeymoon in Oregon's Wallowa Mountains, I lost a rod and reel when I fell in Little Sheep Creek, my mind undoubtedly on other things. In these later years, she thinks I am going to kill myself someday, with an errantly placed shoe on a green log or stone, trifocaled into eternity. Usually her fear for my life means that without strong argument I am not allowed to go fishing unless my sons Lamar and Forrest share the pleasure, or unless I am making a harmless trek up the little creek our cabin borders. What she does not know is that my two sons fish the same way I do. While it is pretty clear to me that they know how I am supposed to behave, and that they watch me pretty closely, the watching is more to know when to pick me up than when to slow me down.

One recent summer I thought I had her convinced that I could still wander off in the mountains by myself to stalk the wily trout. If she only knew. I spend a lot of the time just sitting, paused in wonder at the elegance of nature, traveling away from the streamside task. But I blew it, twice. When fishing with my sons, I had a spectacular fall from a slime-covered, steeply slanted log, tumbling over granite boulders down to a large rock perched dangerously above a pool. I slid down the boulder, and while trying to find purchase where none existed, splashed loudly into one of the best spots of the stream. While they feigned concern, I'm sure it was funny to Forrest and Lamar, and I really did not mind it either. But, they so enjoyed telling the story to their mother—with great embellishment—that she thought I had nearly died.

So, Ardith insisted on making the next trip with me, up the same stream. It all went well, lots of fish on a beautiful day in a wilderness heaven, and no mishaps to suggest I should not be allowed to come back by myself. I even pointed out to her the benign looking spot where I had fallen. After a long and upright day of fishing, we decided to go back to the cabin, walking along an abandoned logging road perched several hundred feet above the stream. This is where I nearly killed myself. The road was covered with grass two or three feet high, and had lots of old timber fallen across it. I stepped off a log onto what I thought was solid ground but which turned out to be three or four feet of air. I twisted around and landed with my head soundly striking a pointed granite rock, producing a cantaloupe-like thunk. It was the first time I can remember seeing not just stars, but what seemed like the whole cosmos. I lay there thinking, "I wonder how long before the pain from the hemorrhaging starts." For her part, Ardith stood there wondering how she was going to get me out, or find the spot again if she had to bring someone after me. I ended up with a big bump on my head, but heredity saved me. Most men of my family are blessed—or cursed—with very large, thick skulls. The real consequence is that now Ardith worries even more that it is not safe for me to go fly fishing alone. I suppose I should start worrying when she no longer does.

Never again to go fly fishing alone, though, would take from me some of the most profound personal riches I receive from the walk along the stream. The emotional wealth I find in fly fishing alone comes not from the self-conscious concerns about exposing my aesthetic shortcomings while distorting the angler's art. Nor do I claim any great gains in personal independence and risk-taking when I am able to wander unaccompanied up the creek.

Fly fishing alone allows me a more open passage between what is going on inside my head and what is outside in the place I fish. My fly fishing in the presence of the disguised disdain of experts, or my wife's fear that I will disappear from her sight beneath the water, are constructed from the intervention of others. These interlopers impose standards not my own on what I do. Fly fishing alone takes away those pending judgments.

It is true that there is a lot to be gained from the social dynamics of group fly fishing. Sharing a common outdoor joy binds one to others in the pleasure of that joint act. The group venture on the stream creates a collective memory, the perspectives on which surpass any individual recollection or even the sum of individual re-tellings. By legend and by experience, fly fishing requires corroboration. The one that got away, or the one that didn't but was sent away, may be reified in the telling, but verified only by the substantiation of others. The creek-side companion is also the logistical backup for the fisher with the forgotten flies, or the broken reel, or the empty tippet box. And, the angling friend is a fount of knowledge and wisdom about what fly pattern is working or not, how deep to let the nymph drift, or how rapid to make the retrieve. These communitarian forays fill a special need for me sometimes, and when shared with good friends and family they add a unique and valued dimension to our relationship.

As great as fishing with others may be, though, there are many times when the act of group fly fishing is inadequate, when it impedes rather than facilitates, when it brings another world into the one that I often want to enter alone.

Alone allows my own pace. I can run the trail from hole to hole, I can leap from rock to rock, or I can spend an hour on a fruitless riffle that provides my fishless joy. Alone, I come and go when I want, and the scheduling of the entry and exit into the stream may be linked only little to the fishing itself, and not at all to the wishes of others.

Fishing alone even completes my personal knowledge of a stream in a way that sharing the space with others cannot. Perhaps selfishly, I always feel that the appropriate niceties of group fishing leave me missing something. What is absent is the exploration of the entire river. When we fish together we alternate spots, or leap-frog long reaches of the stream to ensure that no one monopolizes the opportunities. But I then can only wonder at what it would have been like to stand where my friend stood. It is not simply that I want to catch whatever fish are unavailable to me there. It is instead part of a need for completeness, for knowing each part of the whole, for knowing rather than assuming the flow of the river from one part to another. Moving through all of the cascading water allows a better sense of what binds and shapes those different parts. Moving with the river alone from part to part creates a more intimate knowledge of what is happening there.

Most important, though, fly fishing alone is an automatic, self-opening window into my self. In no way, at no other time, am I as likely to think of things I do not usually consider. Those thoughts surface in a way that I cannot induce of my own will. My mind wanders undisciplined, broaching the unlikely, constructing the impossible. I am not quite lost in thought, but I never quite know where I am going either. I just have faith that I will come out on the other end in some familiar territory.

In some way, I am not sure whether it is the aloneness or the loneliness it produces that leads me to the introspective, untrained self-examination when I am fly fishing with no one else. The solitude provides the door to this interior room, but sometimes the loneliness I find there drags me into it.

It is a loneliness I need, a muffled emotional pain that renews my focus, repairs my sensitivities, and restores my sense of center. It is the loneliness that brings me new understanding of who I am and what I want to be.

4

Lagniappe: The Accidental Finding

"Oh, shit," I mumbled, as one more attempt to deftly place a Yellow Humpie under a willow branch on the far side of Jeru Creek went awry, tangling itself in the matted roots resting just below the smoothly sliding surface. I gently tugged on the line, trying not to lose one of the last from my near-vacant store of flies. My friend Nick Lovrich was a few yards away, a little bit up the stream, himself trying to figure out how to catch one of the crystalline stream's beautiful little cutthroat trout. In Jeru Creek we hope for a six- or eight-inch fish, dream of a ten-inch prize, and rarely catch one more than four inches long.

Nick was barely stifling his amusement at my frustration. But the fly did pull loose, and then gave a brief dance across the surface before it began a short, unguided glide down the creek. The fly had not floated more than a couple of feet when I was prepared to raise the rod tip and lift the Yellow Humpie back into the air for another cast to a safer location. But just as I began to pick up the fly, there was a large swirl enveloping the artificial insect. For a brief window of adrenaline-induced clarity I was hooked into one of the giant (eighteen to twenty-four inch) spawning cutthroat that sometimes lurk in Jeru Creek early in the summer. The fly pulled out of the tender lip almost as suddenly as it had lodged in the trout, and the orange-bodied, hooked-snouted fish lazily dropped back under the willow tangle, apparently unaware or unconcerned of either us or the fly with which we had tempted it.

Strangely, though, I recall no further frustration at the "loss" of the fish. No further scatological expletive echoed the earlier anger of being hung up in the willow shrub. Instead, I remember now only the unanticipated wonder of a grace-filled moment produced by my own error. I know now that just like the thrill produced by the root-captured fly, sometimes mistakes are the best things that can happen. I have learned that looking in the wrong place for the right thing can be an unanticipated blessing.

Error is how we found Jeru Creek, the Pack River, and Paradise—our name for the pools at the upper end of both streams. That finding was a mistake that has blessed our lives for more than two decades. An accidental entry into the wrong office was a portal into new worlds, both natural and personal. It is said that we learn from our mistakes, but that lesson usually is thought to be painful. We have learned a lot from the Jeru Creek mistake, but only rarely has discomfort accompanied it. We have learned about ourselves, about the north Idaho natural places, and about the out-of-place reconstructed society imported from other places. And strangely, it turned out, we felt more at home in what we found there by accident than we did in what others intentionally brought along with them.

In 1976, the year we accidentally found the cabin, Lamar was an infant, and Forrest just two years older. In 1973, only three years before the finding, we had left New Orleans to return to the Northwest. The throat-tightening constrictions of the urban density of New Orleans constantly forced us to dream of the wild country Ardith and I had loved as children. Even earlier than our coming home, in 1970, a five-acre rain forest near Hood Canal—the elegant saltwater L that defines the eastern boundary of the Olympic Peninsula, full of berries, vine maple, and salmon-spawning, spring-fed streams—had emptied our meager bank account.

The subsequent move to the university town of Pullman, though, brought home the reality of hauling a diapered son and his slightly older brother 350 miles across the state of Washington to savor a bit of creation's best. Even if we were able to make the seven-hour trip without the requisite five or six stops along the way, and even if we were able to free time from the many aunts, uncles, cousins, friends, and grandparents, the occasional tented stays in the moss-draped woods served only to reinforce our need for more time there.

So we asked around about where else we might find the "lagniappe" we sought. Lagniappe, in fact, was to become the name we gave our Jeru Creek retreat. Lagniappe is a Cajun term that means a bonus, or something extra, on which one had not counted, and perhaps didn't deserve—but didn't not deserve either. We had a cedar sign carved with "Lagniappe" on it to hang over the cabin door. In retrospect, I should not be surprised at the occasional stranger who wondered if I were Mr. Lagniappe. I do not think they understood when I said they would have to ask my wife to see what she thought.

Some friends in Pullman recommended that we go a little over one hundred miles to the north and look around the country outside of an Idaho town called Sandpoint. Neither of us had been there before. We thought we would look around to see if we could find some property on which a decade or two later we might build a cabin. The first day in Sandpoint it rained torrents. We wandered around looking for real estate agents, and found a few places where properties were listed, none of which particularly interested us. By mistake, we ended up in the insurance office of a real estate company that had its property listings in another office on the other side of town. Because of the mistake, we met a young real estate agent who happened to be in the insurance office also. He described several properties to us, and then said there was one other piece he had but in which we probably would not be interested. He described the property thusly: twenty miles from town, eight miles up a gravel county road, two miles up a dirt forest service road, and a quarter mile along a wooded track to a secluded cabin.

Perhaps as intriguing as the description of the cabin was the picture painted of the man who had built it. Jack Storey was a retired California longshoreman and, as I remember, he came to the north woods to become another Eric Hoffer—the working man's philosopher. I never read anything Jack Storey wrote, but he did a wonderful job of building that cabin.

Ardith and I left Sandpoint early on a newly sunlit morning, and forty minutes later arrived at the cabin, greeted by a stocky tee-shirted man in his late forties, wearing a pistol on his belt. He showed us around the cabin, and while he and Ardith talked I took my fishing rod and wandered up the creek for a while, catching and releasing several dozen very small cutthroat, my success all within sight of the cabin.

At Jeru Creek, I was immediately captured by an environment I failed to expect—a north Idaho rain forest much like the one we had emotionally abandoned on the Olympic Peninsula. In fact, many years later an archaeologist who specializes in the millennial life of the forest actually confirmed for me my impression of the similarity of the two habitats. Since that finding, Jeru Creek has refused to release us.

Lagniappe, the cabin on Jeru Creek

On the way back to town we stopped in at the realtor's office, put down our earnest money, and then returned to Pullman. We never spent another night in the Olympic rain forest.

The cabin itself was a non-descript twenty-by-twenty-seven frame structure. The interior held a single room with a potbellied stove at one end and a Franklin fireplace at the other. The exterior was of a weather-darkened cedar shake, and the roof a corrugated metal with a galvanized finish, installed long before the stylized colored metal roofs of today. Inside, the cabin captured little light, even in the height of the midday sun, providing a dark haven for the many mice that shared residence there. A low ceiling, dark stained chipboard walls, and a few scattered small windows made the cabin seem almost like a cave.

Outside and fifty feet up the hillside was the rustic accoutrement of the less-civilized aspect of cabin living. The "green house," our euphemistically named one-holer, sits just across the road and back in the woods a few strides—initially on land we did not own but subsequently purchased. The green house still stands today, although I have had to replace the cedar four-by-fours that make up the foundation, and a birch tree weighted down by snow once dented the corrugated plastic roof. Each fall we leave Lagniappe thinking that the next spring will require another hole to be dug, but the wonderful restorative powers of nature allow us to retain our usual and accustomed resting place.

Over the years we have made many changes to the cabin. We partitioned one end of the main floor into two bedrooms in order to provide both our boys and their parents some privacy as we all grew older. We added a screened porch on the creek side of the cabin; the porch sits perched over the twenty-foot drop down to the creek, capturing the sounds and funneling them into the cabin through the open window. After pack rats fouled the cabin one winter, we opened up the ceiling over the living area and added a loft over the bedrooms. And, we attached a shower room, replacing Jack Storey's original one which stood alone some thirty feet from the cabin, surrounded by six-foot-high pointed cedar posts, resembling the legendary western military outpost. Still, we must trek to the green house.

But the real draw to Jeru Creek always has been Jeru Creek. In contrast to the shadowy interior of the cabin and the nearly uniform green of the forest, the creek side of the cabin offers a constellation of attractions. The building sits on a rock bluff, perched there twenty feet directly above the crystalline flow of the newly transfused blood of our lives. Jeru Creek is a series of sparkling runs, mini-falls, and translucent pools arranged around granite boulders and ancient stumps, but all in an unexpectedly paradoxical setting. The paradox is born from the fact that the creek lives in a complex, vibrant home with a diverse biological environment. From the back window of the cabin, I count eight different species of conifer, and that occasional spawning trout that has traveled from the lake thirty miles below. Yet—and here is the paradox—there sometimes is a starkness and simplicity to the arrangement of that complexity that somehow brings forth the abstract intentionality of a Japanese garden.

In contrast to the accident that brought us here, the pools, the stumps, the ferns—they all seem carefully planned in an almost sculpted fashion, with a natural elegance and economy to their forms and their spatial relationships. Nature itself has drawn out the essential elements of Jeru Creek, so that the sometimes mystical, and almost always emotional dimensions of our lives there are the lagniappe, the bonus that we know has fed our family, that has nurtured us both individually and collectively, that has provided us with the shared memories that carry us forward.

Lagniappe, our undeserved bonus, is an understatement of the unintentionality of our act that brought us there. Had we not gone into the wrong office at the wrong time to find the young real estate agent, we never would have found Jeru Creek. Our lives would have been different, at least in their recollecting. Perhaps

Jeru Creek

some other stream, down some other road, would have provided us with the same focus of shared affection and experience, with the aesthetic bond and the common context to which we return in our memories and in our dreams. Perhaps the real finding was in ourselves and not intrinsic to this particular place. But I cannot accommodate the belief that there is another place that would mean so much each time we come back. And, in that return, always we come again to the finding, and to its emotion-absorbing, peace-producing wonder.

But the lagniappe for our souls comes from more than the cabin alone, of course, for it is centered in a context that we share with others. The content of that envelope in which Lagniappe is wrapped is both real and imaginary, both physical and metaphysical. It is hard not to find awe and miracle in the fading dusk, with the awkwardly elegant moose edging across the boundaries of the small cedar-sheltered clearing while I play my game with the tiny cutthroat trout of Jeru Creek. And, it is rare to find a spot on Jeru Creek that does not produce that same sense of wonder.

The accidental finding of Jeru Creek and the emotional bounty it continues to provide signaled only the beginning of the discovery of Lagniappe. Sometimes what we unexpectedly find nonetheless meshes well with the growing sense of the jigsaw puzzle pieces we gradually put together as we try to construct a picture of our bonus to life.

What we accidentally found is far more than a stream and a rustic cabin overlooking it. We found a common set of memories and images, each of us shaping them by our own filters and our own needs. As I write this, Ardith and I have left our farmhouse home of fourteen years, and our community of twenty-four years, moving out of the town where our boys became men and we became tolerant of their maturity. Our sights now sit on another city a thousand miles away, itself on the apron of great river-producing mountains, but they are different rivers and different mountains.

Yet, no matter how far we scatter, either in our aspirations or in our lives, nor how infrequently we may return together to Jeru Creek, there remains the constant of our common lagniappe. We know that up that rough dirt road, what we inadvertently found more than twenty years ago will never be lost. In that keeping, Lagniappe will provide the unending, accidental bonus to our memories, and to the lives that created them.

"Lagniappe," Jo Hockenhull, 1999

5

Politics and the Pack

THE PHONE RANG HARSHLY about two in the morning. Hoping to avoid waking our two infant sons, I quickly rolled over to the edge of the bed to answer the call. My adrenaline level was surging and my heart was pounding. I dread the bad news that comes in the middle of the night.

The voice on the other end of the call was faint and fearful, and in a tongue difficult to decipher. I knew it was not family or friend or colleague. In a few seconds I was able to chase away the fog in my mind to figure out who was in need. The caller was Mai Thai, a twenty-year-old Chinese-Vietnamese woman, one member of a war-devastated refugee family that our church had sponsored and for which our own family had agreed to take significant responsibility.

The Thais had arrived in Pullman a couple of weeks before, staying for a while in the home of one of the women of the church until a more permanent place could be found. There were four members of the Thai family: Mai, a small, energetic young woman with an obvious intelligence; her older sister who seemed to have had some terrible experiences that made her much more difficult to get to know and understand; Thanh, the older brother who would soon take on much of the economic responsibility for the family; and Hua Ban, the mother of the other three. Hua Ban was not native-born Vietnamese. She had been reared in China and had been driven from her homeland by the great war between the nationalists and the communists. Hua Ban was of indeterminate age, but seemed well into her seventies or eighties, walking as she did on the traditionally bound feet of the female Chinese.

This family of refugees was not one of the elite allies of the Americans in Viet Nam whose members were rewarded by a privileged place on the airlift as their country fell. The Thais had been residents of refugee camps. Some members of the Thai family can be seen on the covers of one of the American slick magazines of the time, part of that unforgettable picture of the refugee-laden sailing vessel with its terrified passengers reaching out to be saved.

The day of the phone call, the Thais had been moved into a small, two-bedroom apartment not far from the university. They knew no one else in the building, and carried with them only a few clothes supplied by the church and an inexpensive stereo system provided so that they could try to learn English from the tapes they also had been given.

As the night approached, the Thais had gone to bed in their new home, trying to sleep in the sparsely furnished interior, and hoping that the burned-out lightbulb above their door portended no danger to them. As they lay fitfully, they heard a loud noise at the front of the quarters as the lock was being forced. Through the veil of their fear, they knew that there was an intruder inside the apartment, and they could hear him banging around in the living room. Mai, Thanh, their sister, and their aged mother huddled together in the dark of one of the bedrooms, hoping that the interloper would fail to notice their presence and leave them unharmed.

The footsteps soon receded down the apartment hall, out the door, and off into the dark. The Thais waited in silence, fearing that the unknown person would return and do them harm. But the nighttime devil stayed away, and the terror receded. Mai, whose halting English was better than the others, then called us for help, wondering what to do and how to spend the rest of the night safely.

Hoping she would understand, in a kind of broken, pidgin English of my own, I told Mai that I would be right over to find out how I could help. I dressed quickly and drove the five minutes to the Thais' place. When I walked in the front door of the apartment, the fear was palpable. Only Mai and Thanh were brave enough to come forward into the light in the entry hall. Their sister and mother stayed in the back bedroom until they knew they were safe. We talked for a while, struggling to communicate in any way possible, until I finally understood what had happened.

I volunteered to call the police to come, but the Thais refused to let me bring in official help. It took some time before I was able to find out why they wanted no assistance from the police. Mai tried to explain to me that in their Viet Nam and refugee experiences, the police were just as likely to be another threat to them. They were afraid that they would be blamed for the crime, and that the police would offer little sympathy at best, and at worst would bring additional suffering.

The broken lock on the door and the Thais' fear of both the police and the possible return of the burglar left me no choice but to spend the rest of the night on the floor of the apartment, in the hall near the door, placing myself between the threatening outside and the newly traumatized refugees. Early in the morning I called Hal Dengerink, my neighbor and a skilled amateur carpenter. I picked him up, we went back to the Thais' apartment, and Hal put in a deadbolt lock for them.

At no other time were the Thais victimized while they lived in Pullman. Other relatives of theirs came to Pullman, and some of them are still there. But a few years later the Thais themselves moved to San Francisco. Thanh runs a restaurant and Mai works in a bank. We have seen them when we have visited San Francisco, and twenty years later they still send us chocolates for Christmas.

Pullman is not a place known for serious crime, although sometimes it does surface there. And, that Palouse university town is probably as tolerant as one can find in eastern Washington. I do not know whether the Thais were chosen for the burglary because they were politically different, strange, or simply because they were weak and unprotected. I do know that the meanness and the harshness of the reality that produced that nighttime call stunned me then and continues to assault my senses whenever I allow it to re-emerge.

I am no longer certain of the sequence of the Thais' terror and our cabin purchase, but they were close together. And I cannot say that we bought the cabin to evade the kind of fear and failure that event reveals. But, I do know that few reasons for finding a rural retreat were more important to us than our feeling of a need for a kind of psychological isolation. We wanted a place where we could find a sense of mental escape from the nastiness and emotional pain of the morning news and the fear-induced nighttime phone call.

Only a rare location would seem more suited to that goal of escape and solitude than the upper Pack River Valley and Jeru Creek. An eight mile gravel road, followed by a two mile forest service track, and then a narrow quarter mile auto path snaking through the dark evergreen woods is the sylvan course that leads to Lagniappe. Our cabin is itself far beyond power lines, telephone poles (even a cellular phone will not work there), television, newspapers, the daily mail, and the casual visitor.

In that apparent remoteness of the northern woods I was tempted to believe that a natural equality would emerge. I had hope that people, beasts, and botany would be accepted in their mutual contribution to an integrated community. This is a view of the world that some ecological theorists have come to call biocentrism. Through my naive lens, out there in the remnants of the wilderness, intrinsic worth would be the criterion for acceptance. The diversity that we would find in the natural community would be admired and accepted for both its contribution to the survival of the larger ecological system and for its individual adaptive wonder.

As a paradoxical counterpoint to a love of loneliness, though, we found that the Selkirk Mountains seem overrun with all kinds of people seeking that isolation. And I have come to know that the acceptance of diversity, the tolerance of a broader community, the merging with nature as an equal—these are seldom part of the baggage that those sojourners (and perhaps we, for that matter) bring to the Upper Pack River Valley.

In truth, I should have known that the motives for people moving to the mountains are almost as diverse as the ecological world that awaits there. The number of marijuana farmers on the forest lands of northern Idaho is legendary, and those of us who wander innocently through the Selkirk's higher reaches are careful not to surprise those woodland entrepreneurs. Then, too, we sometimes see refugees from the radical politics of the 1960s in their still functioning VW buses, or we catch a glimpse of the rusting buses themselves where they are camouflaged in the growth of the brush around their final resting place. No doubt there also are fugitives from the law trying to escape the promised hard time. There are survivalists who simply want to make do with the least amount possible, and they want to produce it themselves, as they prepare for the Armageddon.

There are California retirees, seduced by the claims of a classified ad in *Outdoor Life*, who came north to finally recover the childhood dreams of an idyllic haven before their own unrelenting darkness. There are gypo-loggers who struggle in their dangerous and demanding labor—battered and buffeted by the large timber companies, the environmentalists, the U. S. Forest Service, and the vagaries of international trade wars. There are prodigal sons and daughters who left the area in their youth, sought their fortune in the coastal cities of the West, and returned in glory or despair, or simply in thanksgiving for the forgiveness of the land. There are the seekers of the alternative lifestyle, who want the security and sanctuary of isolation. There are the airplane pilots, the divas, and the attorneys who claim the valley as their permanent residence, who revel in their earth homes and solar-paneled palaces, but who do not really live there emotionally. And, then there are those of us who are the summer vacation warriors on maneuvers from the universities over one hundred miles to the south. As we venture from the academy to the ecology, we want the best of everything—the reflection of the intellectual life as well as both the communitarian ideal of the pastoral world, and the self-deception of individual victory in the rugged battle with the remnants of an older and more dangerous time.

Yes, even if for quite different reasons, we all want isolation. I know that my family and I at least transiently want to escape from politics, from people, from the events that gradually erode the patina of our shallow defenses against the Thais' experience their first night in our hometown.

But even at Jeru Creek I have come to know that the sense of isolation I sought so badly is only thin veneer. The tranquility is only an opaque film that rarely masks completely a political reality every bit as bitter, as angry, and as brutal as the world that we experienced with the Thais. Perhaps the starkness of hatred is even more evident to me here because of the seemingly untainted backdrop against which it is painted. In spite of the verdant forests, the clear streams, the slow pace, and seeming shelter, I have found politics on the Pack River. There have been politics just over the ridge that separates our valley from Ruby Ridge and the Randy Weavers who used to live there. I have found politics in Sandpoint, the haven for Mark Fuhrman, driven from California by its own politics. And the politics of the Pack and its neighboring valleys can be just as blatant and frightening as that in the Thais' Vietnamese town, in their new found home in the United States, and in the wilds of Washington, D.C.

Race has no equal in America as a historic caustic, constantly grinding down the fiber of those ideals that could have bound together the peoples of the nation. Conflict over race may symbolize religious bigotry, economic dislocation, or cultural dissonance, or an individual's emotional sickness that produces the hatred and the vitriol. But no generation seems to escape the self-damning of this unwillingness to judge others by their person—good or bad—and not by the shade of the wrap. In the darkest times, it seems the iterative inescapability of race and its hatred leads to a sinking, downward spiral, out of which the best we can hope for is an uneasy truce surrounding some pockets of trust and tolerance.

We went to north Idaho with the sense that the peace of the Pack River Valley, Jeru Creek, and our beloved Lagniappe would not generate such dark thoughts. But the truth is even there, and it contrasts even more harshly with the fundamental optimism with which our faith, and our politics, and our love for the valley surround us. The personal pain of this stark reality seems even greater because of the context within which it appears, and the personal way we have felt it. The constant battering of the daily life of the city, or the television-dependent homes that are simply electronic appendages of the metropolis, have unfortunately led me to accommodate even if not accept the frequent violence and racism of the country. But our placid surface life in the hills hides rather than deflects both the best and the worst of the world.

Can I be more forthcoming? North Idaho has a national reputation for being a haven for right-wing, neo-nazi racists. Hayden Lake, the home of the Aryan Nations, is in north Idaho. Hayden Lake is probably some fifty miles to the south of Jeru Creek, but its emotional reach spreads close to our creek-side vacation home. We have been touched by the fear of Hayden Lake, although not by the actions of its residents. The fear was not ours, but that of our friends, and their response has left an indelible mark on our Pack River refuge, on our feelings about the sanctuary we thought was there, and on my own sense of what I am and what I ought to be.

Rob and Louise Tasker and their two children have been good friends since Forrest was in the fifth grade. Rob, a former community college basketball coach, came to Pullman to work at Washington State University as academic coordinator for the athletic department, and since has moved on to other pursuits. Coaching was in his blood, and he took on the task of teaching and developing the basketball talent in the grade schools of the town. His tool was the AAU Junior Olympic program. Forrest played on one of the first AAU teams that Rob coached. From that experience and many subsequent trips to tournaments, including a national Junior Olympic championship tournament in Iowa City, our families grew close.

Louise Tasker is Scandinavian, a five foot, six inch blond former teacher. Louise is a warm, loving and strikingly honest friend. Rob Tasker is six feet, five inches, a world class masters runner, former basketball player himself, former teacher, holder of an M.A. in Sports Administration, now a student affairs administrator in another city, and African-American. The children are the mix of the parents, clearly not the mirror of either mother or father, but a marvelous merging of the two. Rob loves to camp in the wilds.

Rob Tasker also was a career officer in the Navy Reserve. In the summers and on weekends he would go to reserve meetings—usually in Spokane. One summer the Taskers and we agreed that their family would ride to the cabin with us, and Rob would drive from Spokane to meet us after the conclusion of one of his reserve meetings. We left Pullman after work and got to the meadow just off the Pack River road. We found Rob parked next to the locked gate, asleep in his car even while clothed in full Navy dress whites. We woke him and went the final quarter mile into the cabin. We spent a great weekend, hiking to the falls, sitting by the fire pit late into night with the empty bottles of table red on the ground beside us.

When we returned home after the great weekend, we found the haunting newspaper reports of the Friday that Rob Tasker had slept peacefully in the meadow on the Pack River road. Down the river a few miles, near where it enters the valley from Highway 95, the Pack River Road has a series of gravel intrusions into its densely wooded sides. These smaller roads are unimaginatively named A Street, B Street, and C Street. One of the first highly publicized arrests of an Aryan Nation Neo-Nazi occurred on one of those alphabetized streets, just off the Pack River Road, only eight miles from Lagniappe.

Rob Tasker was the first one to call me about the arrest. He said that never again would he go alone up the Pack River Road, even though we all were sure that no harm would come to him. We firmly believed that people came to the Pack River to be alone, but we also held no false hope that these people also rested alone in their racist hate. We just hoped that their intrusions into the valley had made it no farther than A, B or C street.

I do not recall if the Taskers came back to the cabin again. If so, it was only once or twice. I do know that Rob did not go alone, and did not take his family to Jeru Creek without us along. The loss was great, both for them and for us. And we had no control over the fear produced by news of the arrest. We had hoped to provide our own circle of comfort into which our friends could retreat, but at least for the Taskers that circle no longer bounded the Pack River.

Our cabin has been broken into several times. Our sense of violation from the burglary there must pale in contrast to that of the Thais back in Pullman. And, even with no physical violence against us or the Taskers, that dull edge of tension from the shadow of hate down the road never quite goes away. Nor does the anger pass. I feel the anger at the forces we cannot control that drop down through the media to sever the confidence by which our friendships hang. Our sense of helplessness at the inability we have to protect ourselves and friends not just from the harm of hate, but also from the fear of that harm, only underscores the contrast between what we had hoped to find at Lagniappe and what actually surrounds us there.

One weekend, a couple of years after the arrest, our longtime friends the Lovrichs were up at their cabin, which is just down the path a couple of hundred yards from ours. While down in the meadow, which is close to the Pack River Road, they heard the rumble of heavily loaded vehicles. Checking to see if they were logging trucks, Nick and Katherine saw a strange sight: a convoy of about a dozen camouflaged four-wheel-drive jeeps, half-tracks, and small trucks. The machines themselves were driven by camouflaged men, staring straight ahead as they moved deeper into the high mountains. Like a string of soldier ants, the mysterious caravan angled up the road. No identifying marks could be seen on the trucks—no license plates, no insignias, no decals, no little flags.

Nick Lovrich drove his family down the road to Fred and Ellen Lang's to ask Fred if he knew what was going on. Fred knew every law enforcement person and agency within several counties, and at all levels of government. Fred made calls to all of them—law enforcement agencies, federal and state militia and guards, the FBI, and anyone else he could contact. Nobody would admit to any knowledge of or responsibility for the mysterious caravan. Fred believed that either a super secret agency or some non-governmental group that wanted to remain unknown accounted for the shadowy invasion. But, no one ever saw the group return down the Pack River Road, and to our knowledge, none of the federal agencies who flew over and drove in the forests found any trace.

We speculated that one of two things could have happened. The first is that the camouflage really worked, and that the trucks and their contents remain hidden in the canyons and the groves of the upper Pack. I know that whenever I am wandering down one of the old abandoned logging roads, I wonder if the green and brown mottled vehicles are going to appear.

But if the trucks didn't simply disappear into the wilderness, what happened to them? The second possibility leads to another, much more public set of events. There are only two ways vehicles can get out of the upper Pack River: the way they came in, or up over the Pearson Creek Road. The Pearson Creek Road leaves the Pack River Road about three miles up from Jeru Creek, just after the road crosses the river on a steel bridge. The Pearson Creek Road winds up the other side of the steep-sided mountain valley, branches again near Dodge Peak, and then continues over the back side of Roman Nose Peak. Down the other side, the only other direction the trucks could have gone, the road travels a dozen miles to Naples, Idaho, and then back out to Highway 95, the main course north to Canada. Ruby Ridge, near to Naples, is the former woodland home of Randy Weaver who, some years later, for weeks stood off federal officials who sought to arrest him for federal firearms violations, and who lost part of his family in the conflict. I do not mean to imply that the camouflaged caravan ended up at Ruby Ridge. In fact, I strongly doubt it, for the organization required to generate a sausage string of covert vehicles seems anathema to the isolation and individualism of Randy Weaver, at least as he has been painted in the press.

Randy Weaver has his politics too, and they are not mine. Neither are those of the Neo Nazi residents of Hayden Lake, or of the camouflaged caravan of mystery. But what we do share is the false hope of the temporary escape to the politics of isolation—theirs a much more deeply seated and fundamental need to remove themselves from society because of a knowledge of the broad margin that separates them from the politics that dominate. But the politics of the world that require a deep personal involvement also imply a belief in the opportunity to escape from it on occasion, to retreat and reflect, and to come to terms both with the common need for independence and freedom and with the uncommon gulf that would separate our two sets of worldly values.

There are indeed lots of other politics on the Pack . . . the politics of environmentalism and logging, the politics of county roads and the condition in which residents find them, the politics of marijuana growing, of ignored hunting and fishing regulations, of the need to go apart from the world because of a hatred for it and for the change that it is producing. But the Pack River politics that shelter the angry, the fearful, and the hateful also may provide the countervailing energy, the emotion, and the spirituality that produce hope for a politics of a better world. We have not yet seen that collective bridge building energy out of which community is constructed. We pray it is there, remaining only to be discovered and mined by occasional insurgents as well as by those who know no other place.

I still carry the hope of a benign world on the Pack, but just as with the Thais back in Pullman, the fear of our African-American friend, and the specter of the unknown carriers of camouflaged contraband, raise another pain for me. What should be my response? Can I in good conscience ignore the dark side of the life that is barely hidden there? Can I feel comfortable escaping with our friends to the synthetic peace of the Pack River, knowing that it is unreal?

These questions rest uneasily for our generation, those of us reaching political maturity in the 1960s. Of course, members of the '60s generation have had no particular corner on the social equity market, and we have no valid claim to a particular sensitivity to the implications of race-based distrust and fear. While some change has occurred in the past three decades, we remain far short of where we ought to be. The constant personal challenge for me is whether I have done enough, and whether the more that is required should extend even to the apparent peace of the Pack River.

Ardith and I did not march in the great civil rights protests; nor did we go to the Mississippi Summer, placing our lives on the line for our beliefs. But we thought we were not at rest, either, at least in our daily lives. In the '60s, we were told that we were the first white people ever to step into some African-American homes in the rural areas outside of Vicksburg, Mississippi. Ardith taught in the public schools of Washington, D.C., and New Orleans, in buildings where she was one of the very few white teachers. One of the most oddly moving events of my life was at dinner one evening in a hotel in New Orleans. The dinner was a celebration of Christmas by the teachers at Ardith's school. We arrived at the hotel and found our way into a reserved dining room, where we were the only white people present. After a while we were all asked to stand behind our chairs in preparation for the beginning of the feast. The principal called for quiet and then asked everyone to bow their heads in prayer. Then, to my shock, she said, "Dr. Pierce, will you please say the blessing on the meal?" I did, but not very well.

I was told that one of my students was the first African-American male to earn a Ph.D. from Tulane University. I had hope that change was on the way for the traditionally white institutions of the South. Yet, we left New Orleans and moved to the rural Northwest, escaping the turmoil and the mounting racial anger of the urban South. In the more sublime confines of the Palouse Hills of eastern Washington the same tensions had spilled out before we got there. The campus at WSU had its racial strife, and the local county seat was described as a locus of racial hatred in a widely read book by one of the country's most notable authors.

We can recount additional symbolic attempts of our family to make a difference in the way that whites and people of color relate to each other. But I know that it never has been enough, and that there have been those frequent occasions we all face when I step back rather than walk forward, rationalizing my reluctance to take the political risk, suggesting that it would damage my ability to make a bigger difference in the long run, or that whatever issue it happened to be was more complicated than it seemed on the surface, or that we had done our part and it was someone else's turn, and of course, some of our best friends . . .

So, does the past justify the present and the future? Does the memory of the post-midnight visit to a frightened refugee family assuage the occasional timidity of the present? Does a litany of self-congratulated tolerances of the past remove the requirement to do more and again and again and to create a world in which the Taskers can go into our woods without fear?

The answer, of course, is no. There is something about the independence of good works that cannot be ignored. The requirement to do the right thing in the present cannot be mitigated by having done it in the past. If anything, the claim of a history of good works only exacerbates the obligation to do more. Knowing that I fail to answer the call often enough or loudly enough is one of those heavy, jagged stones I carry with me, whether I am walking across a noisy, crowded campus or am nested in the solitary shelter of the apparent harmony of the Pack River.

6

The Sounds of Silence

EOPLE RETREAT TO WILDERNESS in search of silence—a haven from the clamor of daily life. Our family is no different. It is hard for many who are familiar with Pullman, the small, university town in which we lived for so many years, to think of it as chaotic, tumultuous, and noisy, at least in comparison to the great metropolitan centers of the country. Yet, our world has changed a lot. In some very important ways any place where wires or satellites or radio frequencies reach can be just as noisy and boisterous as Chicago or New York or Los Angeles. Not only the physical environment—the masses of people, the car-filled roads, and the crowded sidewalks—has that chaotic character for me. There is a teeming emotional room where I play out both the real and the imagined stresses of the day. It is hard to escape those signs of society that penetrate so deeply into my consciousness, that divert and distort my capacity to sustain calm. So, where is the quiet I pursue?

The trek to Jeru Creek is filled with promise that my search for that silence will be successful. The long, serpentine, rough-surfaced gravel road, the forested archway that leads back into the Selkirk Mountains, the narrow grass track that takes off from the Forest Service maintained avenue—they all do nothing to dissuade me from believing that my time on Jeru Creek will go undisturbed. There is real hope, both in my mind and in my heart, that the refuge always will be waiting. I am rarely disappointed in my search for the forest- and stream-generated sound barriers that wall off the daily dissonance I try to leave behind.

Indeed, the Jeru Creek outdoors seems a silent place, a sanctuary from which to escape the cacophony of social conversation. Yet, even when wandering through the woods alone, I still do a lot of talking. Most of the time I talk to myself, and the monologue or the dialogue usually takes place inside my head. Sometimes the conversations seem quite real, even if I take both parts to them. Other times, though, it is as though my mind's eye is watching a videotape of an event or pattern of events that just recently occurred or that I either hope or fear will take place sometime soon. Still, in all of those, to the natural world outside me there is silence. But, it is not true that all of the time when I am alone in the woods my conversations are silent; there are times when I talk out loud, even when alone, especially when addressing myself after some clumsy mishap along the river.

I do feel awkward when I think I am talking aloud to myself and forget that I have some company, such as my two sons. In fact, much of their early vocabulary to which their grandmother objected came not from overhearing adults talk to each other, or from some shameful adult talking with them. Rather, that foul utterance came from listening to their father talk to himself as he slid down a rock into the river, or pulled a number 10 Yellow Humpie from his ear.

When I walk through the woods—whether it is up Jeru Creek toward the falls or along the old McCormack Creek logging road—and I talk, it's not always because I am lonely or think that I am by myself and have to do something to imitate the social conventions of the more populated part of my world. No, I often have a sense that there are other creatures not far from where I muse. I fail to really worry about those other beings much; I do not fear some yeti-like denizen. To be sure, the odd sweet smells that drift in on the morning mountain windfall, or that suffuse the air late in a musty August afternoon, do suggest the New Orleans gym I played basketball in thirty years ago. But, the animal smells floating around the Selkirk Mountains are not those of the New Orleans gym rat. Whatever their particular source, though, those unfamiliar odors do let me know that even in the remote mountains of northern Idaho, being alone is not part of the bargain, even when I think I am talking to myself.

Once in a while, though, the idea of there being something else "out there" actually makes sense, and becomes real. When that "something else out there" is non-human, I have found that I have no hesitation in actually shifting from talking to myself to talking to the animals.

Along the streams and creeks, of course, talking to the fish is something we fishers all do, but for most of us it is not in real earnest. Fish talking is more like wishful talking, a kind of coaxing of our own capacities, rather than some real sense that the fish are going to respond as urged. Fish talking is more like the kind of banter one hears on the baseball field—"come batter, batter, batter, cuhm batter, battuh, batta" and so on—whose purpose is to relieve the tension of the talker and not necessarily to influence the animal at the plate.

But I have found that there is a real talking to animals that actually works, that makes a difference, that changes the behavior of the beast. Not that the beast understands English, or that I speak "beastlish," but that the emotion and the tenor of the talk carries a message.

One afternoon in August, back when the Fish and Game Department planted trout, I was working through a stretch of water around a favorite bend in the river, just down the road from our cabin. That river reach has a few nice holes, a lot of riffles, and some big boulders—nothing spectacular, but a home water that one can come to know well and fish well with time. Alongside the stream are willow shrubs, right up to the water in the spring, but later on occasionally providing room to walk freely close to the edge and to back cast, albeit with some care.

On that particular afternoon I was fish talking to myself, and I had been somewhat successful. Three or four pan-size rainbow and cutthroat were in my canvas creel. The fish were wet from being dipped in the river for cooling, and they were covered with a blanket of streamside grasses. In the creel, though, the hot summer afternoon weather still mixed the river water with the fish slime to produce a mild smell that doesn't bother the fisher, but forewarns others down wind.

Fish slime odor, though, is not always a warning; sometimes it is a magnet. I was focusing on the river and my low-voiced conversation with the drift of the fly. Out of the corner of my eye I sensed a movement, non-threatening, but slowly approaching me as whatever was there gradually came up the river. I turned, expecting to see another angler, perhaps one of my family or a friend from a neighboring cabin.

Instead, about thirty feet away—staring half-blinded into the sun with her nose up into the wind coming down the river— was a small female black bear and her two cubs. It was apparent to me that mother bear had only one thing on her mind, communicating with the fish in my canvas creel, and that she was tracking on the slimy smell.

In such a situation, I suppose I had some options. One would have been to scream in fear and fury, hoping the emotional expletives would save my life. Another track would have been for me to run, vainly trying to outdistance the bear, or drive it into exhaustion. Or, I could try to hide, camouflaging myself in the trees and bushes with the hope that the bear would wander on by and I would remain unnoticed. I also thought about taking a jump in the river, leaving the bear and her cubs on dry land as I floated away safely. I also toyed very briefly with the option of beating the bear about the head with my fishing pole, a possibility that I soon realized would both be hard on the pole and of no concern to the bear. Then, too, I considered gracefully handing over the fish as a supplicant's offering, counting on the good manners of the bear and its realization that there were no more fish where those came from, unless it wanted to stay around and watch me fish. Alpha male behavior also entered my repertoire of potential response to the appearance of the bear. I could charge it, beating my breast and standing on my toes, trying to tower over it and establish dominance in some fundamental way. Or I could fall down on the gravel and play dead, hoping that the bear would sense that toying with me was a waste of effort. And, in spite of my instinctive reactions I could try to ignore the bear, still fishing while hoping it would just go away.

 I did consider all of those options, even in a brief second. Instead I did what comes natural to me in the woods, or anyplace else for that matter; I did what I do to make my living as a teacher and administrator. I began talking to the bear. I am not sure why, and I know I did not think about it consciously. It was not a scream, or a yell, or that threatening boast with me beating my breast. It was just a brief monologue.

I stood up as tall as I could, and I looked at the bear, and I said softly but distinctly, "I really don't think you want to come this way." The bear heard me, she settled back on her haunches for a few seconds, and then she wandered off into the willows with the two cubs close behind. It turned out to be a fairly simple man-beast encounter, and I have no physical or emotional scars to prove that it happened that way.

I claim no mystical capacity for breaking through the brain barrier of the black bear; nor do I feel as though the bear really cared what I thought. But I do feel that at some base level the fact that I acted without fear, before I had the chance to fear and because fear was not instinctive for me there, and because I acted naturally both for what I do in the woods and in the world—talk, either to my self or to others—the bear also was unthreatened.

This talking down a mother bear is not a practice to recommend. Indeed, since that encounter, I have become more cautious amid rumors of local grizzlies and cougars, as well as stories of moose treeing hikers and ramming pickup trucks. On the other hand, who knows what a few well-chosen words, filling the silence and spoken naturally, and even to one's self, might accomplish when alone in the wilderness.

"Talking to the Bear," Jo Hockenhull, 1999

Instinctively I may fill the silence with my communication with the fish or the bear. Sometimes, though, there is a kind of crushing quiet that seems to overwhelm me when I am alone on Jeru Creek, at least for the first day or two. Ardith and I both have jobs whose days are defined by other people, whose agenda are not often our own, whose phones ring, and whose colleagues query. There seems never to be a time when real silence dominates our work day, or even the work evening. The stack on the desk is high, and never really seems to diminish, the pink slips demanding return calls clamor for attention, and the e-mail signal trots across the screen constantly. It is perhaps ironic, then, that when arriving at the cabin it is difficult for me to deal with the freedom to set my own agenda and to make my own sounds.

It is perhaps that newly found silence in my mind that opens up a heightened sensitivity to the noise around the cabin. The noises are even louder at night, of course, as we rest in our bed with the windows open. For the first few nights, every unpredictable creak or scraping tree limb generates fantasies and nightmares about what is "out there." Is it the militia sneaking up on us? Is it the grizzly bear finally making it over the Selkirk Mountains from its Priest Lake habitat? Is it a drunk who wandered five miles up the road from Edna and Buck's Tavern?

There are real sounds in the night, sounds that belong there. There are also sounds that do not belong, that are the forays of civilization's advance troops, or the straggling of those who have been left behind. And, there are sounds that belong, but that mimic something else, something that is recalled from the deep memory stores, whose paths to the surface are ordinarily blocked by all of the familiar and more contemporary cues.

Even knowing that sounds are strange and distorted and misperceived in the wilderness, it might be a surprise to you to find out that Johnny Cash often serenades me late in the summer. Johnny Cash sings after dark, as I read in bed before sleep, or as I go for my last walk to the outhouse. The Man in Black always sings me the same song, too. He performs that classic, "I Walk the Line." Why he picks that one, I do not know. It was one of my early favorites, to be sure, but I have heard it only a few times in the last thirty years. And why he would want to sing it on Jeru Creek is beyond me. There is no line to walk there; in fact, the lines are all gone. People move to the Pack River Valley so that they do not have to walk the line, so that they can wander all over the place. There is no line on the road, no line in the mind, and almost no line in society's standards, as long as no one else is bothered.

Late in the summer, Jeru Creek's flow is reduced substantially. Jeru drops from a torrent of snow melt to a full mountain stream to a bubbling brook. It is the bubbling brook that seems to sing along with Johnny Cash. It is possible that there is someone with a boom box camped across the creek, back where we can not see them, and where the campfire light is hidden. But, I do not think so. There must be something about the bouncing of the water off the logs and the rocks at a slow deep resonating tone and tempo that mimics Johnny Cash.

The first time I heard Johnny Cash, I was quite startled. I had visited the outhouse just before stumbling back to bed. I stood out on the rock shelf overlooking the creek fifteen or twenty feet below and I listened carefully. I tried to disentangle the voice and the music and the beat from the more obvious tumbling of rocks and rushing of water and air through the riffles. I lingered out there for an hour, wondering if there really was someone down there, and trying to construct a civilized frame for interpreting what I heard. I finally gave up, went inside, and fell into a restless sleep that carried with it a veil of unease about the Man in Black, out there in the dark.

Over time, though, I have come to expect Johnny Cash to make his regular stop at Jeru Creek. Perhaps not so oddly, he comes by about the time of the Sandpoint Music Festival. In fact, I am disappointed if I am not at Jeru Creek when Johnny Cash serenades in the dark. He has missed us a few times, strikingly co-incident with an unusually high or unusually low flow in the creek. And, I miss him when he fails to catch my attention on my evening trek.

I have always believed that the true sign of an emotionally healthy person is the capacity to be satisfied with spending time alone, especially in silence. In fact, for some time my sense of whether we had done a good job raising our children was whether when we went to the cabin they were able to create their own circle of comfort in the silence. I still believe that to be true, that I need to be able to live with myself, to contemplate and meditate, and to accommodate the messages I loop through the circuits of my own mind. I must be honest, though, and confess that I am glad that from time to time a mother bear or Johnny Cash shows up to help me out.

7

Mirage: The Fish that Doesn't Exist

HOW DO I KNOW what is true about myself or the places I live? Must the truth be verified by others in order to carry any weight? Or can I know myself without reference to what others think, crashing on in the conviction that what I know independently is true? As do most of us these days, I live in a space where the standards for truth are ambivalent. The university is defined as the haven for the life of the mind, with analysis and criticism the standard acts. The only truth there is that there is no truth. The academy stands between the inner knowing I hold about myself, and the outer truth I see in daily life.

The uneasy truce among experience, belief, and insight spills over into the natural world as well. Every wild space must have its legends about the great beasts that inhabit it. North Idaho, as in much of the Pacific West, is replete with stories about Sasquatch sightings, or footprints, or odor, or hair left on the upper branches of a sapling on a trail. Many people do argue the presence of Bigfoot. A professor at Washington State University is world famous for his study of Bigfoot. And that professor has been vilified for his alleged attempt to hunt one down and bring back a carcass to provide evidence to the doubters. Others, including almost every other anthropologist I know, broadcast disdain and disbelief at the mere hint of Harry the Sasquatch wandering around in the woods of the contemporary Northwest.

Now, I haven't seen a Sasquatch myself. But, I will admit to wondering about Harry when I walk up Jeru Creek with its narrow canyons, ten-foot-high ferns, and the bad odor that drifts on the breeze. And, when he was in high school my son wrote a poem about an imaginary encounter (at least that is all he admits) with Bigfoot. A portion of the poem follows:

Across the sunlit clearing,
I saw him, half hidden
In the silky shadow of the forest.

You must understand I can't talk
About it because you'd know how true it is;
How true the face
Pivoting like a stranger
In a crowd, fascinated
Caught looking our way.
I must write as if it is an allegory,
But it is true....

On the other hand, I will admit to seeing a fish that doesn't exist. I have seen the fish—not the same one, to be sure, but different examples of the species—many times. Now the fish I have seen is not really that unusual, especially for it not to exist. Indeed, it is a very common, non-existent fish. I do believe, though, that with the years, it is becoming less common and more non-existent. The fish is the Jeru Creek strain of the Pend Oreille Cutthroat that leaves the lake and propagates in the small streams and creeks of its tributaries. These fish are large, especially in the context of the streams they visit, brightly colored, and ferocious when their hook-jawed bodies fight a tight line in a late spring floodstage creek.

For a long time I did not know that this fish doesn't exist, especially after having caught examples of the type a number of times, and having returned them to the creek. That is part of the problem, of course, for much like the Sasquatch proponents, I have no body or carcass, or skeleton to prove the presence of this spectacular trout. In fact, the largest trout I caught (in spite of its non-existence) was two-feet long (really twenty-three and a half inches) and she came up out of a swirling hole in the creek no bigger across than a large garbage can lid.

I will get to the part about the fish not existing in a little bit, but I have to admit that the first time I caught one I didn't know it existed either. During the first spring of our ownership of the cabin, several of my friends joined me for the opening day of fishing season on Jeru Creek. I didn't realize how high the creek would be with snow run-off; it was nearly unfishable, and the large number of small cutthroat that I had caught late the prior summer were hiding themselves deep in the pools.

Nonetheless, we started up the creek and fished for several hours. We came to a spot that later on we would call "travelers' rest," after Lewis and Clark. Travelers' rest is a great flat rock poised above the stream, where we usually take a few minutes to relax on our walks to the falls. I lowered a lure into the big pool at the base of a series of small falls and saw this very large, dark movement toward my spinner. In a flash, my rod bent nearly double. For fifteen or twenty minutes I played the fish to where I could pull it out of the depths. It was a fish to provide hope and inspiration in the early days of our life on Jeru Creek.

What manna! I had found a small stream that delivered dream fish. That was the only spawner we caught that day, but it kept alive the image of glorious futures. Many times in the next ten years we caught others like the spawner...from underneath tangled roots right below the cabin, from Neil's Pool where the monsters lurked behind the big round rock, from Forrest's pool at the very top of our string of property along the creek, from the pool below where the Lovriches now have their cabin.

Several years ago, though, all of us in the Jeru Creek area received in the mail a study by the Forest Service, in preparation for some timber sales in the area. As is required, the case for the sale included an environmental impact statement, with a very brief inventory of the wildlife and fisheries that would be affected by the logging.

I read the impact statement carefully. I was astonished to come across the finding that no spawning fish—the kind I had come to know so well—were present in any of the streams, including Jeru Creek. The result, of course, was that the impact of logging on the cutthroat fishery in Pend Oreille would be negligible.

Certain as I was that these fish actually exist, I immediately wrote back to the person who had signed off on this finding. I asserted the presence of these fish and even offered to take the forestry people with me on a trip and catch some for them.

I received no response to my comment on the environmental impact statement. It is possible that the Forest Service experts continued in their belief as to the non-existence of the fish; more likely, they extrapolated from the fish to me, believing that anyone who argued the presence of a non-existent fish must not be real either. Now, crudely following Descartes, because I thought, I thought the fish existed; therefore, I thought I was as certain as to my own existence as I was of the existence of the fish, but, at that point I did not see fit to argue either case.

It is strange, though, what effect an official statement has on one's convictions. Since I learned that these fish don't exist, I have caught no more of them. Actually, my attempts at catching them have dwindled substantially.

My increasing reluctance to stalk these beautiful creatures may have a couple of sources. I think one is a real decline in their numbers, especially since new neighbors have been dumping tree trash in the creek, building artificial barriers to the migrating spawners.

But, I think it also is true that there is a kind of mystical withdrawal from a fish that officially is not there. How can I catch one if there aren't any? And if I do catch one in the first place is it not likely to increase the probability that it will not be there in the second?

Perhaps, most important, is that I failed to carry the argument any farther with the Forest Service. I had this funny feeling that proving the presence of the fish may in fact be the biggest step possible toward eliminating it. If I went public, and demanded agreement that the Jeru Creek giant cutthroat really is there, wouldn't the world know? And, if the world knows, it would come to Jeru Creek, and the fish soon would no longer be there. And then there would be the tragic irony of a non-existent fish being eliminated once it is clear that it really was there.

Well, is there a moral to this story? Not really, at least not for the fish. The moral may be for poor old Harry the Sasquatch, who once it is clear that he exists, will no longer.

Lamar

8

The Survivalist

THE EXACT DATE escapes me now, but I do know that Lamar and I were driving to the cabin for some trout fishing in Jeru Creek and the Pack River. We were crowded into the front of our little red Dodge Ram pickup. Our Basset Hound, Nellie, was tightly cramped between us. We were off for a family weekend. Ardith was planning to drive up later because I had asked her if just Lamar and I could make the ride together. For some reason, I had decided that it was time to talk with my younger son about some serious matters. As I recall, Lamar was about sixteen, close to entering his junior year in high school. We were long past the facts of life, those having been more or less effectively transmitted by friends, his older brother, the schools, our doctor, and the well-intentioned, undoubtedly awkward advice of his parents. Instead, I had come to the conclusion that now was when Lamar needed to decide who he was and what he believed. In our family, believing in something is very important.

While the timeframe is fuzzy, I do remember clearly the location, and the situation. We were on our way to Sandpoint, Idaho. We had traveled about forty-five minutes out of Pullman, just north of Potlatch, Idaho, on U.S. Highway 95. About where a little country Methodist church sits not too far from the first rest stop going north, I turned to Lamar and asked, probably too gravely and too bluntly, "Son, what do you believe in? What do you really care about?" Perhaps he thought I wanted to challenge his religious beliefs, or that I wanted to create a situation where I could confront him on whatever he might say to me, or that I wanted to intervene in his own most private thoughts. But the real question I had in my own mind was whether he believed in anything at all. I am not sure why I thought this was the right time to ask, either in the trip or in his life. As I think about it now, I am certain that I could not have said anything of substance in response to the same question at the same age. And, sure enough, he heightened my adult anxiety by his refusal to answer. Lamar sat there, across the nylon seat, slightly hunched and his face turned away, as far away from me as he could get in that narrow little cab. He was wondering, I am sure, why he and his uncritical, unquestioning dog were held captive.

In retrospect, the irony is that even then Lamar believed quite strongly and very deeply about a lot of things. One of those beliefs was that they belonged to him, and it was his choice whether or not to reveal them. In hindsight, if I had considered carefully his life to that point, I would have understood the core character of those beliefs. But I was more bound up in my own fatherly quest to pin down his adolescent ideology than in an open entry into his surprising maturity. I have since learned that now, as the adult into which he has evolved, we cannot get him to stop talking about what he believes and why. He has beliefs about anything one can think of as a topic of conversation: sports, music, economics, religion, science, business, people (including himself), and politics. His beliefs are strongly held and not obviously modeled after any of the rest of us. He claims to be a social liberal and clearly is humanitarian, but sometimes he also postures as an economic conservative. He is seemingly blind to color, political location, hair length, intelligence, or nationality as the measure of the man or woman. He searches deeper, for a fundamental goodness and a tolerance by others of his own unique constellation of views and of his own assertive way of making them known.

In the years following the ill-chosen pickup pilgrimage, Lamar and I have grown much closer emotionally. To be sure, we are strong-willed holders of our own beliefs and often unwelcome arbiters of each other's actions. We sometimes still will find ourselves intensely and angrily on opposite sides of issues, but not often are they political or social disputes. We have our disagreements in the political arena, but we find an emotional pleasure from the banter and the intellectual tussles that economics and politics produce. Usually, when we come to those rare verbal blows it is over how one or the other of us ought to behave, usually in relationship to someone else in the family; then the pleasure retreats. In calmer moments, though, we can laugh at our parodies of ourselves in argument. I make my points to Lamar with my brow furrowed, my eyes intent, and, most typically, with my right arm partially extended in front of me, jabbing home my point into his chest. Lamar, in response, or even in aggression, stands with his arms spread wide, hands cupped, but moving forward and back gesturing in time with his hard-toned oral argument, while giving the physical impression of being at great loss as to why he must make his obvious points so strongly.

With time, the frequency of those father-son encounters has greatly diminished. The more I have let go of controlling Lamar's life and overtly monitoring his beliefs, the closer he has come to me and I to him. Ironically, I guess, the increasing trust I place in him to make his own judgments about both his life and mine seems to elevate his view of my capacity to advise and counsel him. Nonetheless, I cannot help but still feel compelled to place my boundaries on his behavior; as much as I try to restrain myself, I cannot keep from believing that I know what is best for Lamar's life. I also know that they are my boundaries and not his, and that Lamar understands that he can cross them at his own will, even with knowledge of the pain the trespass causes me. Perhaps, though, precisely because my boundaries for his behavior are now more easily permeable, his standards seem to mirror more closely his father's values.

I have been writing about a father's attempt to capture the beliefs of a strong-willed son, and our gradually converging views of the world. So, perhaps my effect on Lamar has been powerful after all. But I know that it is not that simple. We have a term in our family that sounds scientific but really is not, at least as far as we know. The term is "retro-genetics." Given all of the time the people in our family spend in rivers, one would be forgiven for thinking that retro-genetics is an evolutionary phenomenon, one where we gradually turn from people back into fish. But that is not how we define the term; for us, retro-genetics refers to the process through which parents inherit traits from their children.

It is not surprising that many of our friends have seen significant similarities in the values, attitudes, and behaviors of me and of my two sons, especially those of Lamar. The assumption held by others usually seems to be that I have had this profound influence on him, structuring—if not controlling—his development into the man he now is. And, as the pickup trip suggests, it may be true that especially in the early years there was a strong strain of my trying to recreate myself in my sons, not as I am but as who I want to be. But those few people who really know our family well, who have seen the evolution of our collective character over time, understand that in the last half decade especially, Forrest and Lamar have had as much influence on me and who I am today, as I have had on them.

There was a clear turning point in the retro-genetic process of influence between generations. That moment remains one of my starkest memories of Lamar's time in our home. It was later in the same year of that tension-filled trip to the cabin in the little red pickup. That turning point marked the clear inception of this recursive influence in my relationship to him; it was where his influence on me began to be as profound as my impact on him.

In itself, the event was of no great moment, clearly not at the time anyway. As I have implied, it had become clear to us that, as he grew older, Lamar was developing a very strong personality. Lamar was struggling pretty effectively with the task of developing a niche for himself in a family that already had three members with some success and forceful, well-defined selves of their own. Lamar was following an older brother who already had established himself as a gifted musician, a fine student, and an able athlete. And, in retrospect, Lamar also may have been suffering from a father who wanted him to be like his older brother. But where Forrest may have internalized his resistance to my attempts at parental control, Lamar emerged more visibly on the cusp of rebellion.

In the autumn of his junior year in high school, Lamar started doing things his own way, intentionally becoming the risk-taker in a fairly risk-aversive family. I must confess that I reacted to his growing individuality in a negative, authoritarian way, wanting to keep him in line and on the road to success my way. But Lamar would have none of that; he may not yet have known clearly who he was, but he did know who he did not want to be—neither me nor Forrest, at least by our doing.

One evening that particular fall we were having a heated discussion after dinner. We were in the family room, near the parquet counter that divided the space between our living area and the kitchen. The disagreement that night was over whether Lamar was being responsible in his homework (which he never seemed to have). He wanted to take the family car over to see a friend, and it was a school night, and he had some tests the next day. In that argument, as it grew more fierce, I had this painful and rather obvious revelation—the differences between us really were not over whether his homework was going to get done, but over whether I was going to be in charge. And, it was clear to me that I might win the short-term battle that night, but we had come to the point where I could lose the more important relationship for the long run.

Through the dark clouds of our anger, I quietly said to him, "Son, I love you too much to risk losing it. I am going to leave it up to you to make the choices about your life and how you run it. We still will hold you responsible for the consequences, especially in how they affect other people, but it is up to you to decide how you are going to get there." That was not easy for me to say, and I do not know that I really meant it, but the threat of the lost affection of my son pulled that concession out of me.

I would be disingenuous were I to suggest that I lived up to my end of the bargain with no exceptions. Ever since that evening of anger, though, Lamar has been increasingly willing to take responsibility for his own life, to invest in informed risks and to accommodate the consequences of failure. He has taught me much about the importance of risk taking, not for its own sake, but for the greater value it might realize. Some of the biggest changes in my life, including the decision to leave a community and a job of twenty-five years when I could have been sliding into retirement, and the choice to embark on a book of personal essays that reveal much more about me than I really want others to know, reflect the model that Lamar the son set for me the father.

In the years since that family room encounter, Lamar continues to be a risk-taker and a survivalist. He is a survivalist because he accommodates failure and defeat in a way that allows him to define the possibility of another success for himself. For me, I must admit that it remains a struggle not to give him unrequested advice or not to guide him to take the direction I would have him travel. It is hard to let go, but that is the risk I have taken as well.

His risk-taking bravado, and his analytical and critical mind sometimes bordering on arrogance, mean that Lamar can seem to have a hard, tough, cavalier exterior. Where I have learned much from him, though, is not just in the risks he takes. Where Lamar continues to instruct me more profoundly is in his instinctive, compassionate, emotional investments from which he gains nothing. Without obvious rewards, Lamar commits himself to the risk of carrying others' despair, their pain, and their suffering.

I think the first time I should have recognized the depth of Lamar's ability and commitment to respond to those in need was when he was in the eighth grade. Early one gloomy winter evening, I left our restored farm home to drive the mile and a half into town to pick up Lamar from where he had spent the early evening with his friend Eric. Eric was a kind of outsider in town, what some people thought to be a fringe type, and a nascent artist who sported long hair and later on a goatee. He and Lamar were friends on the periphery, as they seemed to meet some special needs in each other. For Lamar I think Eric provided someone with whom he did not compete in another arena, who would allow him to be who he wanted to be, and who also provided a safe haven for Lamar's desire to be a little different from the rest of his family.

Eric lived in a small home on a tree-shrouded side street in the oldest part of town, appropriately called Pioneer Hill. I turned off the main street going up the hill and into the dirt alley that led past Eric's house. As I came to a stop, at first I could not see anyone, and felt some irritation at Lamar not being ready for me. Lamar and Eric then emerged from the shadows down by the house. The two teenage boys were talking in quiet tones. Their heads were slumped and their demeanor downcast. In a few minutes Lamar turned away and walked slowly up to the car where I was waiting. When he settled in the seat beside me, I asked him how Eric was doing. I knew that Eric's mother had a quite serious and rapidly deteriorating case of Multiple Sclerosis. Lamar sat there quietly for a few seconds. Then he said that a few minutes ago he had been there in the room with Eric's stepfather and his mother, when she died. Lamar knew her death was imminent. Rather than do the easy thing, to escape to his own home with the reassurance of healthy parents, Lamar stayed with Eric. What characterizes Lamar best is that staying with Eric and his mother was not a choice for him, it was not conscious risk-taking behavior, not a chance to do the right thing.

Staying with his friend was what Lamar did instinctively; he did it as a matter of course. This deep compassion has bonded him emotionally with a toddler in our church, struggling with cancer-ridden eyes, and sent him into the middle of a swarm of killer bees in Acapulco to protect some other children. Beneath the intellectually tough exterior is the instinctive empathy for those in need that characterizes much of Lamar and his life. But, there is also the belief in his own beliefs that shows up beyond this compassion of his and allows him to act without self-consciousness.

Perhaps in no way in our family has Lamar more exhibited both his compassion and his emotional toughness than in his closeness to his Grandmother Pierce, my mother. She, too, was tough while instinctively serving others with compassion, and with little obvious reward. And she always seemed to have a special place for Lamar inside her brittle shell, especially in the last year of her life. Partly, she wanted to make sure that Lamar was never lost in the shadow of his precocious older brother. Partly, too, it was because—more so than in her other grandchildren— in Lamar she saw herself. And, partly, Lamar responded to and communicated with her in a non-obvious way that the rest of us failed to recognize, at least at that time.

It was Lamar, too, who was closest to my mother in the final months of her life. She began to fail early in 1995, while Lamar still was a junior at the University of Puget Sound. He and Amanda (later to be his wife) would occasionally drive the twenty-five miles to Yelm for Sunday morning church services with his grandmother. Lamar would accompany Amanda on the piano while from the traditional hymn book she sang a solo in the tiny, rural church. Later in the evening, mother would call us full of pride and love at the gift they had provided her and her friends in the church.

The Sunday visits to Yelm allowed Lamar to recognize the terminal decline in mother's health in a way that we could not in our distant weekly talks with her over the phone. That summer

Lamar decided to stay on the west side of the mountains, working in Olympia, while Amanda came to Pullman to live with us while she worked and went to summer school. Lamar lived with Larry and Gail Schorno, childhood friends of mine in Yelm, driving the twenty miles to work in Olympia each day, and sometimes helping out on the farm. The Schornos themselves were daily caregivers to my mother.

But Lamar also spent that summer with his grandmother, nearly every day stopping to see her, doing odd jobs around her house, and listening patiently to her complaints about the family and the community. Lamar had the capacity to listen to my mother's aging bitterness and still retain his compassion. He peeled away mother's veneer of anger and depression and established an unarticulated emotional link with the frail old woman. It was to Lamar that mother gave her wedding ring, for him to give to Amanda.

After we felt compelled to move mother out of her own home into an assisted living place, Lamar spent even more time with his grandmother. The care center was a five minute walk from the ranch where Lamar stayed with the Schornos. Lamar's daily reports of his visits and of mother's decline brought us over to Yelm to move her back home for the final months of her life.

Watching Lamar and mother in that last year of her life has led me to reflect on my own relationship to my grandmother when I was only a few years younger than he was that summer. Grandmother Berdine moved to Yelm while I still lived and went to school there. Mother cared for her, stopping daily at her apartment in town, and later on seeing her in the same care home in which my mother herself spent her penultimate months. During my senior year in high school, grandmother still lived alone, in a small but neat three-room apartment in the middle of the little town. Grandmother Berdine could no longer walk the few blocks to the post office to pick up her mail or to the store for her food.

Every school day, save for the occasional trip out of town with one of the high school athletic teams, I would spend the forty-minute lunch period with grandmother.

When the bell ending fourth period rang, I would bolt from the two-story, brick-faced school, run down the exterior stairs, hurry downtown to the post office, pick up the mail (Box 284), and walk the block off main street to Grandma Berdine's apartment. Lunch would be waiting for me, and Grandma Berdine would feed me at her small wooden table in the kitchen, usually having prepared some unseasoned combination of cottage cheese, boiled beef, or chicken and Franco American spaghetti. We would talk for a few minutes, I would read the *Franklin County Sentinel*—the hometown newspaper from Nebraska that grandmother still received each week—and *The Reader's Digest*, focusing most intently on the anecdotes in the humor sections. I then would rush to make it back to school in time for the first afternoon period, half jogging up the street, past the town's only grocery store, taking the short cut across the railroad tracks and past the Assembly of God church into the brick schoolhouse.

I am not exactly sure why I spent that time with my grandmother. Surely the visits partly came from a sense of obligation, and a fear of hurting her feelings should I not appear once the routine had been established. In retrospect, I probably was avoiding the social exclusion I felt in high school. I was active in school sports and lots of other activities. But I also felt isolated socially, and spent many a Friday and Saturday night at home. So, at least in part it may have been ordinary teenage anxiety and social unease that drove me to the refuge of my grandmother's boiled beef. There was waiting for me a safe and welcome environment in her apartment, and, too, I could sense that she needed me. It was the right thing to do, but maybe not entirely for the best reasons, at least not solely for the kind of reason that seems to have led Lamar to his grandmother.

So, I have learned a lot about myself by the introspective contrast to my son, Lamar. I remain impatient with myself. I also remain impatient with Lamar. I try to mirror his willingness to leap out, and I try to resist the temptation to structure his options so that he more closely mirrors me, or at least what I want to be or I would hope to be. But, Lamar is his own person, and few places reveal that independence more than does Jeru Creek and his experiences there.

Lamar is a risk taker, but always with substantial consideration of consequences. He, more than any of us, has taken off by himself, or sometimes with a friend, into regions where he has never been before. The destination may be a tiny creek high in the Selkirk Mountains or a little town on a remote Greek island. The result is that he often comes back with the most unusual experiences. One of those unique encounters along the Pack River was with "the survivalist."

Survival seems a goal of almost everyone, so it always has seemed a little strange to me when I run across someone who calls himself a "survivalist." I wonder about the alternative—would that be a non-survivalist, a euthanasiast, a thanatosist, a Kevorkianite? And, I wonder about why someone would adopt that label. Just what does survival means for these people? Is it survival of a way of life, or of the body alone?

Lamar, twenty years old at the time, was an inveterate explorer of the nooks and crannies of our river and creek valleys. While Lamar is reasonably and cautiously realistic about the odd mix of people who share this terrain, he also is willing to engage almost anyone in a conversation if that person has something different to say. This penchant to talk and listen with little threat to anyone provides Lamar with some unlikely experiences.

One of those striking incidents happened one summer when Lamar encountered a self-described survivalist in one of the Forest Service campgrounds that span the entrance to a ford crossing the Pack River. The campground is down the road a couple of miles from our cabin, and Lamar was off on a solo fly fishing adventure into a place we call "The Forest Primeval." Lamar parked his car at the campground where it is easy to ford the river, got out of the vehicle and wandered over toward the rocky shoreline. Off to the side Lamar saw a tent, with an old rusty green pickup parked beside it. The truck had a gun rack showing through the back window, and National Rifle Association decals stuck on the glass and the bumpers. In the heavy, steady rain, a camouflaged, shadowy figure slowly emerged through the dripping veil of the tent flaps. The unshaved, brooding man carried a rifle and wore a cap with Survivalist stenciled in black across the forehead. In north Idaho, the woods are full of idiosyncratic people, and idiosyncratic groups of people. This survivalist announced to Lamar that he was from Hayden Lake, known locally as the home of the Aryan Nations. The Aryan Nations is a self-avowed racist organization with a large compound at which training and educational sessions take place.

After a few minutes of talk about the weather, and suspicion-laced inquiries about Lamar's intentions, the survivalist asked Lamar if he would find their location on the map he had with him. The survivalist had no idea where he was camped, at least in relationship to anyplace else. Lamar, who since childhood has captured maps in his memory, including all of the topographical ones of the upper Pack River Valley, readily agreed to look at the unfolded, creased sheets. Lamar's observation, kindly put (and without intentional metaphor), I am sure, was that the survivalist was not on the map. Well, the survivalist said, I am supposed to go to the Upper Beehive Lakes for five days, with three days of food, and survive off the land. Lamar responded that the Beehives were not on this map either.

Lamar, increasingly worried about the fate of the survivalist, asked him what he intended to eat for the other two days at the

Beehives. Holding up his 30.06 rifle, the survivalist indicated that he intended to cook plenty of squirrels. He apparently had not thought about just how much of the squirrel would be left after it felt the rifle's brunt.

Lamar said that he had to be getting on with his trip up the creek, and he would see the survivalist later. He added that the survivalist really should get an appropriate map and some more food. The survivalist responded that instead he thought that maybe he would go into town and get some beer. He asked Lamar if he would like to come along. Lamar declined, whereupon the survivalist asked for assurance that Lamar would not steal any of his camping equipment. Lamar said, no, he had no need of that equipment and went off across the river, entered the forest on the other side, and explored his new space for the rest of the morning.

When Lamar returned from the Forest Primeval, the survivalist was gone—tent, rifle, and pickup alike. Figuring that perhaps the armed Aryan had located the Beehive Lakes, Lamar went back to the cabin, reporting on his adventure to the rest of the family. Later that day, we decided to drive to town. About five miles down the road from the cabin is Edna and Buck's Tavern, right where the Pack River Road bridges the river. Parked at an angle outside of the tavern was the survivalist's pickup. It seems that the survivalist had figured out just how far he had to go to get his beer, and he didn't need his rifle to kill the can.

Now, the question is this, What about this survivalist? There is a tendency to conclude that he was unable to even figure out where he was, why worry about him and his friends and their survival? He obviously was uninformed, and we hope incapable of doing anyone, much less the squirrels, any harm.

On the other hand, maybe the strange, lost man really was a survivalist. He came quickly to know that he was unable to make it in the natural world, and what he really needed to survive was a tall cool one before he hit the road back to the compound. In the

Lamar and Forrest

end, survival was not necessarily going it alone in the wilderness for whatever personal or political reason. Survival was this particular outcast making the rational decision, given his own limitations. He knew his limitations right away, with a little help from Lamar, and he knew what would help him survive within those limitations—a glass of beer in a warm, welcoming bar.

So, then, what does this story say about Lamar? I have said that he, too, is a survivalist. He seems to have a knack for knowing his limits, and the limits of his aspirations. When his aspirations exceed his capacity to achieve them, he more than survives, he flourishes. He lays out new goals, he rationalizes his failures, he absorbs the pain, he forgets about the disappointment, and he strikes out again. Along with his strong beliefs and his instinctive compassion, Lamar also is partially defined by this survivalist nature of his—the taking of the risk, the occasional success along with the frequent failure, the survival, and the energy and the hope to try again.

The survivalist encounter also unmasks the counter-side of Lamar. Sure, he was willing to take the risk of direct interchange with a man who by his own declaration of his politics and demeanor could easily have been a threat. But knowing Lamar as I now do, I am convinced that this instinctive openness to the Aryan Nation survivalist expressed the same character as the compassionate boy who stood with his friend Eric at his mother's premature death, or sat with his grandmother as she welcomed her onrushing escape from old age and infirmity. I have tried to learn this from Lamar, the risk-accepting subjection of my own self-interest to another's need, but I know full well the dimensions of my frequent failure. I know too that the silent, sullen teenage boy in the red pickup on the way to Jeru Creek already had well in place the kind of character I had no need to shape or judge.

So, as I go deeper into the later years of my own life, I try to let go, both of my own caution, and of my need to protect Lamar from his incaution. But even when I think I have made it to where I can say that Lamar knows best about his own life, that he can make his own choices, and that he is willing to live with their consequences, I find that I still want to manage the boundaries of his survival. So, I pray now that as I become more comfortable with the unknown hazards of my own choices, I will be more willing to let Lamar live with the jeopardy of his.

9

Masquerade

THE RIVERS I FISH rarely are what they seem, nor are the people that frequent them. The beautiful creeks and streams of the Pack River Valley hide pain-generating drop-offs into which I often have fallen. When I return from treks up Jeru Creek from our cabin, I often bring with me the physical evidence of those hidden perils. By the end of the summer my arms and legs are scratched and scarred from trying to maneuver up and down the rocky, brush-sided, timber-strewn course. Knowing that there is going to be pain from those trips does nothing to dissuade me from entering the creek each time I search for the emotional salve that comes as well.

Sometimes the disguise someone brings to a relationship is a deception that creates grief, damaging and distorting my expectation of pleasure and reward. Other times, though, my not knowing what lies behind someone's unseen mask makes no difference at all, even though the charade is an elaborate one designed to harbor secrets about which I would not care. And, I have no trouble identifying those times when what I saw is not what I got. Nonetheless, the illusion out front provides the opening through which I have gained access to another mix of life with both its joy and its sadness.

I am reminded of the thin, socially constructed veneer that overlays us all, and especially those who are important to us, every time I sit down to write at our cabin at Jeru Creek. The cabin is twenty feet by twenty-seven feet, with two small bedrooms at one end, and a vaulted tongue-and-groove cedar ceiling that carries over the living room into a small loft above the bedrooms. A four-by-six picture window looks out from the main room, peering down in a Cyclopean way at Jeru Creek some twenty feet immediately below.

In front of the window, abutting the wall, and lodged just under the sill, sits a table. The table is six feet long and three feet wide, made out of closely matched one-by-twelve pine boards. The planks are glued and planed to a point where the beginning of one edge and the end of the other are nearly indistinguishable. The table top sits on a rectangular base of four vertical two-by-fours.

The surface of the table is a honey gold, the outgrowth of years of conversation among the natural aging of the pine boards, the discoloration of the lacquer finish, and the rubbed-in remnants of multiple coffee spills. Fanning out through the pine are plumes of amber, creating patterns that provoke Rorschach-like interpretations of their meaning. That table is a cabin constant; it is always there, waiting for our re-entry each spring. The table is a solid reminder of where we are and why we are there, and perhaps most importantly, a connection to the past that put us there.

Grandpa David made that table for us. Not long after we bought the cabin, he showed up with the disassembled pieces stuffed in the back of his little red hatchback. The table was his contribution to our cabin Lagniappe, his gift a kind of reparation for the past and a legacy of love for the future. The reparation was not required, nor appropriate, at least to our minds, but the legacy has lasted, both as a reminder of Grandpa David and a lesson of the masquerades that can both control and enrich our life.

I suppose the human masquerade may be more appropriate on the river than in other more socially dominated parts of our lives. Especially to the fly fisher, successfully presenting the unreal is the goal, is the pleasure, is the standard and not the shame or the secret. Perhaps it is in that context, of the river and the art and the artisan, that it becomes especially clear that the unspoken can remain the unknown if we want it to, and the unspoken and unknown can be unimportant because there is no choice. That was the case with Grandpa David.

Grandpa David was not really a grandfather, and to my knowledge never a father—at least in the biological sense. He has been dead for more than a decade, taken by a stroke while in his early sixties. Grandpa David was about five feet, eight inches, heavyset with a protruding stomach, and very little hair above his ears. He wore glasses, and often was clothed in khaki shorts that revealed a pair of oft-injured knees that hobbled his ability to hike his beloved mountain trails. A Stanford Ph.D. and former public school administrator and college professor, David spent his last few years in a small frame home in an industrial section of Portland, surrounded by warehouses and backed by a mosquito-infested drainage ditch. He lived with an adopted son, a young man he had met while teaching at a college in the Midwest. Grandpa David talked a lot, and claimed to know almost everything. He loved to eat, to cook, and to travel. The physical attributes of this highly educated but superficially plain old man belied his intellectual depth and his emotional complexity, and disguised the secrets that he withheld from us only half-heartedly.

I first met Grandpa David at a church camp, a couple of summers after my father had died. With several new friends, I was walking down a narrow trail from the main hall to our sleeping cabin. This bald, paunchy guy, wearing tan shorts that revealed those scarred, knobby knees, called to us to see if we would be willing to help collect wood for the evening campfire. I volunteered to help, and from that action connected with Grandpa David for the rest of his life.

Grandpa David was, at that time, a school administrator in a small northern Washington logging town where he lived with Pearl, his eighty-year old mother. Pearl herself was a special person, having ridden as a young woman across the Cascade mountains on horseback around the turn of the century. In the summers that followed that first meeting, David and I would hook up on church sponsored camping trips, usually in the

Olympic mountains. Sometimes along with other people from his town we would take his boat into the small islands between Vancouver Island and the mainland of Canada, or up Lake Chelan to Stehekin into the North Cascades area they love to call the "Norway of America."

On one trip, Grandpa David almost died from bee stings while hiking along the upper part of the North Fork of the Sko-komish River. We had scaled down a fairly steep grade off the trail into a series of plunging pools in the river. Long before I had taken up fly fishing, I dropped salmon egg-draped hooks deep into the bottom of one of those pools. In short order we had caught a half dozen twelve to fourteen inch rainbow trout. We hiked back up the side hill through the trees when he kicked up a ground nest of yellow jackets. I didn't know he was allergic, but it soon became clear. He barely made it back to the camp, which was about a mile and half away up the trail, to where he had some medicine. He didn't move from the sleeping bag for more than a day, and there was a period when we did not know if he was simply sleeping or was sliding away from us.

After I finished high school I went on to college in Tacoma, and several times Grandpa David drove the three hours to campus for a short visit. One time he invited me to go to Mexico with him and a friend of his, Jerry, but my mother refused—for what reason I did not know. But he brought me back a rough-hewn silver cross on a chain, which long since has been lost. All of this time, Grandpa David seemed to have little or no social life outside of the school and the church. Certainly he seemed to have no female friends outside of the church and his job, although he told me the story of once having been engaged to be married, and then having the engagement break off at the last minute.

I am not sure when I first had the hint that Grandpa David was homosexual. We never talked about it, and in all of the church sponsored trips in the mountains and the boat trips to the San

Juan Islands, if true, it was a carefully hidden secret, masked by his strict adherence to convention. I do remember the first time I took Ardith to meet him. We were not yet married, and we were on our way to Vancouver, B.C., to visit her aunt and uncle. Ardith was (and still is) a tall, beautiful, and intelligent blonde. I remember sitting in David's small living room while he was elsewhere in the house, and I picked something off the bookshelf to read—it was a collection of ancient Greek essays about love among men. During that brief visit it also was clear that there was a surprising kind of negative tension in David's reaction to Ardith—to be sure, this is a kind of retrospective interpretation overlain on hints of subsequent knowledge.

We all went on with our lives, and I went to graduate school in Minnesota and Ardith and I married, and Grandpa David drove three hundred miles to our wedding and grew to love her like the daughter he never had. When David died, he left Ardith his mother's jewelry and the handmade quilts she had sown in the early part of the century.

In our second year in Minnesota we heard from David that he was moving to St. Paul to teach for a year at a local college. It turned out that he had been fired by the very conservative local school district in Washington. The reasons we were given for that dismissal were vague at best, having something to do with reduction in administration during a time of financial stress, and I always wondered about what had really happened. David stayed at this new school for a couple of years, and then moved on to Indianapolis to teach at another small college. There he met the college age young man he later adopted as his son. Then, not much later, David was separated from that job as well, we were told for being too liberal politically for the conservative Christian school. David and his newly adopted son moved to Portland, where they scraped by on his retirement and social security until his son could finish school and find a public school teaching position.

During that period our own first son was born, and we gave him the middle name of David, and David himself became Grandpa. At various times over the years, until his death, Grandpa David would come to visit us and his namesake, as well as Lamar, Forrest David's younger brother. Grandpa David would bring us presents, but of the kind that again belied the hobbled and grizzled looking old man. On the walls of our old farmhouse home two of those gifts, original Chagall lithographs, hung with uncommon grace and beauty. Those lithographs are sculpted with some of the same distinctive floating, mystical forms as those honey-colored wraiths in the pine table that Grandpa David gave to us not long before his death.

Grandpa David, with Forrest and Lamar

The omnipresence of Grandpa David's pine table at the cabin in some ways stands in contrast to an earlier commitment he had made to us when we bought a piece of property on the Olympic Peninsula. When we lived in New Orleans, and thought we might never permanently return to the Northwest, we signed a contract for five acres along a stream that flowed into the lower end of Hood Canal, an elongated elbow of Puget Sound. We agreed to buy the property in collaboration with Grandpa David. We would take responsibility for paying off the contract, while he would reimburse us for half of the monthly payments. After the first year, we received no additional payments from Grandpa David, a budgetary consequence of some seriousness for the meager finances of our young family.

Grandpa David never told us why he stopped making the promised payments on the Hood Canal property. He also never told us he was homosexual. And, we never asked about either one. The Chagalls in our house, our son's middle name, and the table in our cabin tell us that neither one really mattered. They also tell us that even while some masks are always left in place, with time they surely lose their capacity to hide the real person behind.

10
Flylife

THE POWERFUL ANALOGY between fly fishing and the vagaries of life flow through almost every work I have read of the particular genre of writing that I have come to call "Zen fishing." I know very little about Zen. I do know, though, that whether it is *A River Runs Through It*, *The River Why*, or *The Habit of Rivers* there is a temptation to not only see parallels between life and fishing, but also to draw deep and meaningful lessons from experiences on the stream.

What are those alleged parallels between life and fly fishing? Perhaps the most clear is the notion of cycles, of life and death and surge and decline. Obviously, the great periods for a human—birth, death, mating—are paralleled in the fish, and even more dramatically so, as they are not overlain with the social constructions designed to disguise them. Rivers run deep, we know by platitude, and so does the human psyche. Hidden rocks and unplumbed depths stand as unknown obstacles to both the successful float and the healthy life.

The river goes through seasons, swelling and shrinking, each period playing its own role in the larger ecological dynamics of the natural system of which it is a part. Our own lives have these "ups and downs," these psycho-rhythms and bio-rhythms that bring us to the heights of our time, and drop us into depression and despair. Fly fishing itself combines the false with the real in a way that we see in our everyday life. The artificial fly, designed to imitate the real, is not unlike much of how we relate to others, as we try to construct from our own behavior an impression of ourselves we want held by friends or rivals.

Just as in society, fly fishing has its ethics which are more or less held by and conformed to by the people who participate in it. The catch and release, the respect for property, the tolerance and space given to others who fish, the sense of a collective good that needs to be preserved—these all are similar to the kinds of values that often are prescribed for healthy community lives. People who fail to hold to those values are treated with considerable scorn and derision, both on the river and in the pages of fly fishing literature.

But, is fly fishing really another paradigm for life? Can we take fly fishing to be a purified model of the daily choices, the priorities, the processes that confront one each morning? Is the choice between a barbed hook and a barbless one fundamentally the same kind of decision that one makes in remaining faithful to a spouse, or in dealing with a customer? Does the beauty of the sunset-silhouetted back cast provide the funnel into a person's soul? Is the stalking of the trout, the taking of the fish from the stream, the return or the killing of the mottled creature by the deception of the dry fly, really analogous to the primitive need of humans to fend with nature? Does the purist's approach to fly casting really represent the highest calling?

The answer to all of these questions is quite simple: "Not really."

Columnists may decry the rude behavior of boorish fishers who intrude into the streamside space of anglers already present, and we all have experienced the unthinking caster who thrashes a pool with a gang-hooked lure while we wait for the stream to rest. But, are these behaviors "unethical"? Not by my view. Or, if so, at such a level as to trivialize what I could call "true" ethical acts. To me, the judgment as to ethical or unethical behavior needs to be reserved for the core values of a society, not for its social niceties, even if those niceties are ignored far from the normal urban social context. For me, ethics has to do with issues of fundamental morals, and with the crucial questions having to do with life and death, and the conditions under which those take care. Ethics has to do with the central dimensions of relationships between people, and between species, not with the veneer that has been laid over those relationships that serve our personal interests and pleasures.

Does that mean that it is inappropriate to apply ethical standards of behavior to people's conduct while fishing? No, to the contrary, when fly fishing there are lots of ethical issues we confront in ourselves and in other people; they just are not the ones that have to do with who has the right to get in line to the hot steelhead hole. (I will admit my belief that the boors who jump in line ahead of other people may be the ones more likely to engage in fundamentally unethical behavior, but I have no evidence for that.) The ethical issues in fly fishing really have to do with our core treatment of the resource which we exploit for our personal pleasure as we fly fish. The issues have to do both with the impact on the ecosystems themselves as independent and valuable elements of the world, and with the secondary ethical implications for the preservation or destruction or alteration of that resource for other people.

If fly fishing is no metaphor for the ethical conduct of life, why then do I have such interest in those "Zen fishing" books, the ones that take personal experiences and reify them into larger-than-life meaning and symbols?

Some of these works are elegant descriptions that are a pleasure to read simply because I appreciate the aesthetic quality of the language and the story. I would read these books even if the author had written about something other than fishing. Fishing is just a vehicle for the artful construction of an organic word structure in which the parts feed each other, growing into an object of beauty. The fishing is irrelevant in a substantive sense, but not as an instrument to the art. Fishing is the artist's nude body in repose on a divan, the subject for a verbal palette to show one's skills and one's pleasures with shape and light and color. Fishing—the fish, the fisher, the environment, the stalk, the success and the defeat, the joy and the frustration—provide for some writers, and for their readers, art for art's sake, not for the sake of the fishing.

I read the Zen-fishing story not simply because the events that occur and are described are relevant to fishing, but because they call out other emotions for other situations that emerge in the fishing story. The relationship between man and woman, among men, between father and son or daughter, between man and dog—these all can occur in contexts other than fishing. But something about the fishing theatre elicits an understanding of those complex relationships because I can identify with the situation itself. It is not that fishing is the critical subject, but in fishing there is a stimulus to the clarification of relationships. The fishing context as described by the literary artist becomes a catalyst for the focus on a more purified identification of the experience. Perhaps it is because the fishing context seems simpler than others; the natural environment of fishing reduces the number of human actors on the stage. The events that occur while fishing need not be fishing relevant, but can call out other emotions. And, when I am motivated by the search for insight it is those other emotions in which I am instructed by the Zen-fishing work, and not in fishing itself.

The Zen-fishing story is a fantasy, a dream place to which I aspire, and which I cannot describe or imagine myself. The writer of the best work of this genre has the capacity to create the unreal for me, to articulate a possible world that I had not yet brought to focus in my own mind. It is hard to read some of these books without a sense of longing for a real, concrete experience born from the one I know can exist only in words, or in the pictures those words paint in our minds, and before that only in the mind of the author.

The Zen-fishing story also is a better description of something I have experienced than I could fashion myself. The literary reification in the colorful and insightful work causes to emerge those dimensions of meaning I only faintly have found in my own understanding. I come from reading the artistic formulation of something akin to an ordinary moment in my own life with an "ah ha, that's what that meant" or "that's why I remember that." And by revealing the quality at the core of some prior experience on the stream, the Zen-fishing writer forces me to come to the same stream or to each new river with a different eye, an eye that is more connected to the mind than the one that is simply and ordinarily an extension of the fish-seeking, rod-holding hand.

It is not only the written word that strikes at my imagination, that causes me to look forward to what I hope and backward to that which I did not understand. Our home has a lot of "fishart," an oblique aesthetic arm of Zen fishing. The fishart is in frames on the walls, hanging as a mobile from the ceiling, sitting on tables, swimming on the bottom of a teapot, wrapped around a flower vase, decorating the handles of pewter spoons.

This collecting is partly just that—collecting things that are unique referents for a central part of my emotional life. Perhaps because I grew up in an early post-depression home, I have always had a longing to hoard something of value to me and to others, to have a body of objects that make some sense both as individual elements and as part of a relatively integrated whole. As objects are added, a collection provides evidence of accomplishment. A collection provides a boundary and an opportunity for defining what objects appropriately reside on each side of that boundary. And, a collection provides a focus of accomplishment that deflects attention from the frustrations, disappointments, and defeats of occupation.

Collecting fishart is partly accidental, as friends and family gift me with something they know I will appreciate emotionally, not only because of the gift itself but also because the giver knew me well enough and cared enough to add to my soul. In my own case, it almost was if I discovered one day that I had a collection, but with no real intention. In that sense, the collection was a consequence of my life that was expressed both in the way that I acquired for myself, and in what others acquired for me.

Partly my collecting is the reflection of the artist, who not only contributes to the world of art, but who as friend and colleague has contributed to my life, to the richness of the world I experience emotionally as well as visually. My friend Jo, who is part of this book, is such a person. She taught me many things about art and about important parts of the social and political world. She gave me a very large drawing, after I had rather uncouthly admired it on the wall at the university. It is black and white, pen and ink I think, and about three feet high and eighteen inches wide. An umbrella-shaped tree is at the center. But the tree is a woman, and the tree canopy is formed from cosmic symbols. The tree roots are the feet of the woman, and they walk on the back of a mature salmon, itself bounded by script saying "we cross the waters to a new life." That work now hangs at home, on the wall behind me at my desk, a constant reminder to me of Jo's fundamental goodness as well as her incomparable artistry.

And partly the collecting is the self-aggrandizing gift from me to another, but it is something I want and value in my own life. It is no surprise to anyone in my family when my wife Ardith opens a gift from me on a special day—Mother's Day, or Christmas, or Valentine's Day—and finds an object d'fishart. The family room in our Pullman home was fronted by glass windows covering a space of about fifteen feet wide and thirteen feet high, looking out on the highway through the trees and facing into the mid-day sun. Hanging down from one of the window frames was my 1992 Mother's Day present to Ardith—two three-foot long translucent salmon, one above the other, separated by several feet of string and off-set vertically, anchored by the wicker fish basket used by my father years ago, and now counterbalancing the salmon by holding several heavy rocks.

The fish are variegated, multi-layered in color, only a quarter inch thick, and a little exaggerated in the crook of the snout. From outside, with the light from behind shining through, the fish gave the appearance of languidly swimming in an outlandishly over-sized aquarium. The light reflected off the surface of the fish much like the fleeting sparkle when a trout turns on the bottom of the stream. Ardith was honest with me when she opened the Mother's Day gift. She didn't like it. The fish are contorted in shape and color, and fish are not her thing, and these are not particularly motherly. Now, though, she says she has grown to love them, for their deceptive elegance as they swim, for their kaleidoscope of colors teased out by the changing lights, for her knowledge that I too love them—although perhaps for all of the other reasons that she does not.

Fishing contributes richly to the emotional, mental, and physical dimensions of my life. Art and literature rest on my walls and shelves and those works evoke choices about self, others, and the environment. I feel my own need to write my own words about the river. How then can I say that fishing is not a metaphor for life and for the ethics that should govern it?

The answer is that there remains a gulf between what I sense to be the elemental attributes of my life and the insights that the writing, the art, and the fishing itself ink on it. River fishing is fun, it is instructive, it is inspiring, it is challenging, it is frustrating, it is religious, it is profane, it is disappointing, it is depressing. But river fishing is not life, nor is it the perfect paradigm for it. Even so, river fishing surely makes my own living much richer.

The author in May 1947, with the largest trout caught in Alder Lake that year.

11

The Inclined Plane

"I NEED THE PIPE WRENCH from the basement," my father muttered. He was on his belly, wearing his striped coveralls, stretched out on the damp, concrete pump house floor. He lay there with his right arm wrapped awkwardly around the cast iron head of the pipe that sucked up and sent water into the house. I knew full well that the simple statement declaring his need was an order for me to get the wrench.

I trudged my reluctant eleven-year-old body into the gray Northwest drizzle, up the slightly inclining, now soggy yard. I entered the house, tracking mud across my mother's linoleum floor. I went down the wooden stairs into the old basement, with its rubble floor and coal bin, and rummaged through the drawers of a dresser serving as the family tool box. I found the pipe wrench at the back of the bottom drawer, hidden behind assorted screwdrivers, hammers, and planes. I hauled myself back up the stairs and through the house, stopping for a quick cookie and some milk, and then ventured back out into the rain, across the wet grass, and down to the pump house. There I presented my father with the required pipe wrench. With a grunt from his supine position he took the jagged toothed tool, clamped it on the pipe where it entered the pump itself, and started to give a twist. Then he looked at the exposed wiring going into the head of the pump and said again, "I need a screwdriver." So I got up off my haunches and once more headed out into the fabled Northwest October rain.

I do not remember the rest of that particular afternoon. I am certain, however, that like many other weekend winter days, I repeated that trip through the rain to the basement a dozen times, and the pump surely started up again and water must have flowed into our old farmhouse. What I do remember clearly, though, is that my family expected all of its males to be like this memory of my father, omni-skilled, having the capacity to do anything and fix anything needed to make life work. This was not an easy burden for me to bear. My natural inclinations were not in this direction, but rather toward ideas, aesthetics, and athletics. And my father's early death two years later abruptly interrupted whatever intergenerational process of teaching and learning about wood, wiring, and plumbing might have taken place in spite of my bent elsewhere.

During my first grade in school, we moved to a five-acre piece of prairie, underlain by glacial-based gravel moraine that covered the layers holding the water drawn by the pump my father was trying to fix. We had a couple of small outbuildings, a four-acre fenced pasture, a small well, and several gardens. My parents were dustbowl refugees from Nebraska, having lost to the elements a small farm on the banks of the Platte River during the Great Depression. My mother's father was a small town blacksmith, and my father's father a climate-threatened farmer himself. Both grandfathers were self-reliant to an unusual degree, as one had to be in those troubled times. Father came to Washington a few years earlier than mother, and I was born a few years after she arrived, right in the middle of World War II.

At first we lived on the dairy farm on which they both worked, father driving milk trucks and mother cooking for anywhere from ten to forty people. Initially, we stayed in a two-room, outhouse-backed log cabin, a remnant from the days of settlers. But after the log cabin burned down from an over-heated stove, we moved for a short time into a single-room, dilapidated "bunk house," and then into the town of Yelm, where for a couple of years we rented a small home built from the large glacially rounded granite fieldstone that littered the prairie.

Then, when I had started first grade, my parents were able to scrape together the down payment for the five-acre place where one or more of us lived until my mother died forty-five years later.

The author's childhood home in Yelm, Washington

The house had been the home of the Clarks who had unsuccessfully tried to start a truck garden on the rocky soil. Their hopes had been elevated by a local irrigation district which had distributed Nisqually River water to berry and vegetable growing places around the area. The irrigation district soon collapsed and the Clark place came up for sale.

While mother and father held reasonably secure and stable jobs—he still was driving milk trucks and she had obtained an emergency teaching certificate—the memory of the lost Nebraska farm and the lingering threats of the depression experience drove our life at the new place. There was a fundamental, unspoken belief that we had to remain self-sufficient, that we could not count on those jobs, and that we had to be able to feed ourselves once things went bad again.

We engaged in many home-based ventures in our drive for security. We raised chickens, buying 500 chicks and growing them to the stage where they were ready to be sold as fryers to the local processing plant. We always kept out about fifty for ourselves. Mother taught me how to kill the fowl by ringing their necks, or by placing their heads under a two-by-four, stepping on the wood plank, and separating the head from the body, all of the time dancing to avoid the spewing blood as they ran around headless. And, it was then that I learned how to pick the pinfeathers from the scalded carcass, readying the chickens for the freezer or for canning.

For a couple of years we also raised two or three hogs, kept in a small pen down by the shed we called the "barn." Reflecting our need to recycle, the pen itself was built from abandoned boards used to construct the wooden flumes that had carried irrigation water to the place years earlier. I do not remember why we abandoned the hog growing, but I was glad when I no longer had to go down to the barn to feed them early in the morning. In the pasture we raised a beef cow or two, and at the end of the season they would be carted off in the crank-started pickup to the farm where we had lived before, slaughtered, and then carried to the local meat processing place for cutting, wrapping, and freezing for storage until we reclaimed them for dinner.

We also grew our own hay out in the field. The pasture was planted in clover and orchard grass. Because of the reliable rain there was no irrigation, although the remnants of the old water-carrying ditches still striated the fields and our back yard. My father bought a used John Deere tractor for working the field and preparing the gardens. The two-cylinder tractor had a plow, a disc, a harrow, a rake, and a mower. We only needed to borrow a baler, again from the farm where we used to live, to bring in the hay and stack it in the little barn. The John Deere used a crank to get started. I soon learned not to wrap my thumb around the crank when starting the tractor if I wanted to keep that thumb operable, as the kick back from the crank could be powerful.

Stopping that tractor was even more challenging than getting it started. I also learned to bring the machine to a halt by shifting it into second gear and driving into a pile of boards nailed to the floor in the barn. Sometimes I took a plastic-handled screwdriver and carefully ground the engine on the block and one of the two sparkplugs.

My first and only venture into machinery work was on that tractor. Late one summer, after my father died and I had entered high school, I tried to keep the various activities of the place going, plowing the garden and harvesting hay in the pasture. But the clutch went out on the tractor, and we could not afford to have it replaced by a mechanic. So a neighbor (Jerry Noonan, who eventually became a professional mechanic) and I decided to rebuild the clutch. We took it apart and went downtown to the Brown Brother's garage, which had the local John Deere parts catalogue. When we found the part we needed we knew we did not have the money to buy it. So, we had them weld some spots on the clutch plate so that something would engage when we pushed in the pedal. We then put the clutch back together. There were extra parts left, but the clutch worked—although from that time on I had to come to a complete stop whenever I wanted to shift from first to second, or second to third. We sold that tractor when I went off to college, partly to help finance the first semester's tuition.

We raised rabbits for a while, keeping them in a small set of hutches attached to the backside of the barn. I remember eating a few of them as a child, and, with some reluctance, affirming how much my former pets tasted like chicken. I also remember when we stopped raising rabbits. One day I thought I would help them out by picking some special grasses in the front yard to supplement their ordinary pellet diet. The next morning they were all dead. I do not know if the grass killed them, but I was convinced that I was the perpetrator—something I never revealed to my mother.

We gardened and we canned—beets, rutabaga, carrots, corn, peas, and tomatoes—and we harvested bushels of knobby potatoes, distorted by the rocky soil, that we then stored in an abandoned well cellar about ten feet down in the ground. I had the misfortune of retrieving our dinner staple all winter from the damp, moldy, and eventually rotten pile of spuds. We also had a small orchard—a half dozen apple trees of various varieties, some cherry trees, hazel nuts, and pears. Fall always brought the obligatory trek into that orchard to pick the fruit for canning.

That house into which we moved during my sixth year required constant attention. The furnace was coal fired, with the coal truck coming every couple of weeks. I got to shovel coal into the hopper, and carry out the clinkers and pile them in the back yard, until we eventually put in an oil furnace. The wiring was old and the interior was in bad shape. My father re-wired the house and put sheetrock on the walls—often late at night, doing all of the work himself. He replaced much of the plumbing as well. Father worked long hours driving the milk truck, and then would come home and work on the house while my mother carried out the traditional chores of running a household after having spent the day teaching. I developed the image of my father being able to do anything—fix the tractor, wire the house, plumb the bathroom, install the wall board, and solve every other problem that might come along. Many years later, that ability to be self-sufficient remains the model of what I think I should be able to do and the source of my frustration when I am unable to do it.

After my father died, my mother, sisters, and I tried to pick up where he had left off. My mother did not want to be dependent on anybody in the town, and I did not want the town's people to think that I could not be the "man of the house," since that was the first expectation one of my uncles had instilled in me the day my father died. So, we tried to keep the gardens going, more or less successfully, and we harvested the orchard. As I recall, we raised chickens for only a couple of more years, and the property never saw another hog or rabbit. We fixed the fences, replaced pipes, and put in new fuses when the lights went out. I mowed the lawn and drove the tractor, sometimes converting the plowing into time trials for racing around the perimeter of the pasture. We kept the house in pretty good shape, and if we could afford it, when anything major came along we hired Grampa Noonan to come over and work on it.

After I left home, my mother continued to repair and replace when needed. And whenever I came home for a vacation, or dropped in on a business trip to the area, she would have a list of things for me to do—sometimes as simple as replacing lights she could not reach, but other times more complicated and time consuming.

The real lasting legacy of the Clark place, though, is the sense that I too should be able to fix anything—electricity, plumbing, tractors, and more. The frustration is that I cannot, especially when we are at the cabin, which is like my family's early homes, basic in plumbing and power, with the need for constant attention and repair.

Unfortunately, when I do my own work on the cabin, without the help of someone more skilled, I have noticed that I cannot divorce my approach to carpentry from my academic and scholarly constructions. I wander around doing my other things and have a germ of an idea or image tucked away. Gradually, the germ grows and a fuller but still fuzzy image forms. I work with the image in my head for a while—a verbal or written image for my academic work and a more visual or pictorial one for an addition or change to the cabin. The image changes, is edited, even before it is set with pen or hammer. Then, when the image has become sufficiently clarified, I try to produce a rough draft, a sketch of the entire project, in a single sitting. So, if I have the time to write I sometimes will draft fifteen or twenty pages in a day, to try to replicate that whole grasped somewhere in the farther reaches of my mind. Then, I go back and fix things—take pieces out, expand or change, or sometimes discard entirely.

The problem with my cabin construction is that I build rough drafts; I am in a hurry to get the framing done so that I can tell whether the physical model approximates the mental one that I have used as a guide. I forget that the costs of change are so much greater in cabin construction. And unfortunately, the cabin rough draft is not so easily taken apart and put back together. When the frame is not quite square but the plywood siding is, and it is cut and nailed before noticing that what fits perfectly at one end is a quarter inch off at the other, I despair. The mistakes are cumulative, and the consequences of change magnify. But, at least, the frame can be covered, and the error in the early draft of the screened porch, or the shower room, sometimes can be hidden. Still, I know what lurks underneath—not a revised draft, but a covered draft, and that draft falls far short of what my memory tells me my father would have built.

At Jeru Creek we build and repair incrementally, until we reach a crisis point, at which time we may do something more ambitious. Even in crisis, though, there is always the strain between collective action and more individualized implementation of change.

You may wonder what all of this has to do with the principle of the inclined plane that serves as the title to this piece. When Nick and Katherine Lovrich were building their cabin, we all pitched in to help. The less we knew about construction the more we were willing to help, and to offer advice. One of the early challenges the Lovrichs faced was how to get the roof beam in place, creating the ridgepole to tie together the two ends of the cabin thirty feet apart. The two end walls had been constructed and they were erect, held in place by braces toe-nailed to the cabin's plywood floor. The roof beam had been nailed together, fashioning overlapping two-by-tens or two-by-twelves which, when joined, stretched the length of the cabin.

The obvious question then became how we were to raise the roof beam. We did not have the capacity to lift it externally by a hoist or pulley. It was too heavy for one person to hand carry an end of it up a high ladder and place it in the end wall notch. We sat on the plywood floor, drinking beer, and pondering the possibilities. The sun was shining and the beer was pretty good, and none of us—save for Nick and Katherine—felt particularly distressed by the beam on the floor rather than on the roof. Then, along came Neil—my wife's brother. He is not an engineer, although at that time he worked for Remington Arms and Dupont. He was a psychology major in college, and had been an artillery officer in the Navy, neither of which trained him in roof building. More than anything else, though, he is a problem solver with a biting wit. His immediate and almost enigmatic response to the quandary we faced sitting there on the uncovered floor was "the inclined plane."

Oracle like, "the inclined plane" was all that Neil said before he wandered off down the creek-hugging trail that led to the meadow and on to the road. We were left to sort out how to use one of the great principles of the world. In a time span long enough as to be somewhat embarrassing, we had an idea, and it worked. We collectively lifted one end of the roof beam to the lower end of one of the angled ceiling joists for the framed end wall of the cabin. We fixed that end in place so that it would not slide back down. Then we lifted the other beam end onto the angled joist for the other wall. Then we "walked" the roof beam up the inclined plane, alternating very small steps on either end of the beam, until it slid more or less easily into place in the notches prepared for it.

While not even a modestly revolutionary insight, the inclined plane worked. In the intervening years, "the inclined plane" has become a code phrase among the families at Jeru Creek, especially when we face a problem. However, we have come to know several things about the solutions to such problems. The first is that they will take us some significant amount of time to figure out, and many frustrations will emerge, the expression of which will depend on which of us is carrying the load for achieving a solution. My frustrations tend to be more verbal, expressive, and unrepeatable, especially when I forget the difference between doing a rough draft of a paper and a rough draft of a building project.

The second lesson is that very often the most we can hope for is a proximate solution to our problems, not the perfect one. Almost everything at the cabin that poses this kind of conundrum is unique for us; it is the first time we have faced the problem, and it probably will be the last. Even if a challenge recurs, it has been long enough from the first time for the solution to have been displaced in our memories by some other rough draft. Thus, apart from a couple of our friends who are particularly compulsive, we have no major investment in getting it (whatever the task) done exactly right, or the best way, or the most efficient way, especially if it can be covered up later. Our investment is in getting the task done, period, albeit without significantly damaging the little community's aesthetic sensibilities. I have found that learning how to do something really well in order to do it only once is not how I want to invest my time, in spite of the imperative of my post-depression conscience. This offends some family and friends who somehow expect our fabricated intrusion into nature to result in the same perfection as that already present there in the stream, or in the conifer canopy. Yet, for some of the challenges I face at the cabin, even getting a solution done—period—is a major investment of time, energy, and psyche.

The third lesson of the inclined plane is perhaps the most important, and the one that I can carry with me out of the Pack

River Valley. When faced with a seemingly insurmountable problem, whether in building a cabin or in staggering through the obstacles of daily living, I know the best solution is to keep focused on the basic principles. Those basic principles help me find a solution. The solution may not always be the most elegant, or the most efficient, or the most praiseworthy, but it will be a solution, time and time again. And, it will be an answer to which I can be reasonably confident that I will return even if the same or similar problem crops up again.

Perhaps that is why I return to Jeru Creek, to Lagniappe, and to the basic problems that face me in filling a water tank, moving a roof beam to its place at the peak of a cabin, or helping a dead pine find its way to the wood shed. My time there forces me to reconsider what I have claimed as my basic principles, my reasons for being there, and for being with others, and to affirm those principles by which I want to live when I return to the outside.

I sometimes fear that I will lose the lesson of the inclined plane when I am gone too long from Jeru Creek, especially now that we have moved a thousand miles away. And, I do not want to contemplate the possibility that our family will revisit the dust-bowl and depression necessity that forced my mother and father into the model I sometimes try to emulate. But the work I do on the cabin does reach down deep inside me to link my adulthood with my youth and with my father and the model he set. That connection is one reason why Jeru Creek and Lagniappe rest so deeply in the store of memories that I carry along with me, memories both of watching my father, and of being a father. And that is why the gift of the inclined plane travels far beyond the north Idaho woods.

The Falls

12

The Forest Primeval

OUR WORLD AROUND JERU CREEK is full of places we have named, but these are names that mean something only to those of us who are part of the family cognoscenti. I think our younger son Lamar probably has named more places than any one else in the family, although it is not always exactly clear as to why we call things what he called them. Sometimes the names have emerged out of someone's enthusiastic or not so enthusiastic description of an experience in the mountains (Paradise, for example). Sometimes they are the social euphemism, disguising the true nature of the place (such as the Green House), and sometimes they are the recollection of another name in another place.

Nonetheless, the names guide our conversations with each other and they give us a kind of secret language. These family labels provide the referent and stimulus for pulling from our inner mind the memories that mean the most to us, and tie us the most tightly to this place and to each other. Along with those retrieved memories comes the recurring realization of the emotion, if not the reality, of the time and the place that created them.

One of those places with special meaning is what we have come to call The Forest Primeval. My journey to the cabin is both metaphoric and physical. Not only do I try to escape the stress of the present, in my mind's eye I see myself traveling back to the time before I existed. I search for a place undisturbed, even by my own presence. I want to find that unknown destination where I am the stranger, the interloper who is observer without altering the observed even as I stand there. What was it like before I came? And, can I know that? Even my being there ensures that what I see is unlike what was there before. I know that no virgin valley waits. But for me, up the Pack River and not far from the cabin there is one place where the feeling of the first discovery, of unauthorized entry, of a different time seems to cast its shadow. And the shadow is literal as well as figurative, for the descent into the "forest primeval" is one from the light into an eternal mid-day dusk.

Many parts of the Pack River Valley have been logged a couple of times, the first late in the prior century or early in this one, and then again some time in the 1960s or 1970s, or they have suffered nature's own toll. The most recent of the acts of God in the valley was the Sun Dance fire of the 1960s. The Sun Dance fire started over on the Priest Lake side of the Selkirk Mountains and swept over the peaks and down across the upper Pack. The fire came within a literal stone's throw of where our cabin now stands, although the cabin was not yet constructed. The rain forest lushness of the Jeru Creek canyon and the wind direction kept the fire from jumping the creek. But all up and down the valley above Jeru there remain the gray splintered spires of the Sun Dance fire. When we first took ownership of the cabin, in fact, it was almost as if an eruption had occurred, prescient of the photographs of the devastation evident in the early-post Mt. St. Helens eruption era.

As part of our touring of the local streams, hunting for the fire-ignored woods or the creek nobody else fishes and still laden with trout, we came across what we have come to call The Forest Primeval. On our map we saw where Pearson Creek empties into the Pack River. It is down the road from us about a half mile, and across the river from a campground, and there is a faint recollection of a ford to cross the stream late in the summer. The outfall of Pearson Creek into the Pack River is barely noticeable, looking more like a small spring than a respectable creek. But the map showed the rivulet stretching back up into the mountains for several miles, originating in some ponds high on the other side of the river valley. So, we took our fly rods and some huckleberry buckets, crossed the river, and went in search of the unseen trout.

We walked up an old logging road for a few hundred yards, and then decided to drop down to the creek, which we could hear only faintly. Brush grew alongside the road and hid the view down into the creek valley. But when we pulled aside the brush and started down into Pearson Creek I was startled by the change in the physical and emotional aura of the place. The hillside above us was only spotted with occasional red-barked pine trees and the hill floor was covered with huckleberry bushes. The brush veil on the creek side of the road, though, disguised a passage into what seemed an earlier time.

Little light filtered down into the creek bottom, for towering cedars screened out the sun. Only a few plants—a fern here and there, an Indian Pipe, and an occasional Devil's Club where the ground was damp—emerged from the needle-covered floor. The creek is small, dropping down a continual series of tiny falls into shadowed and shallow pools. The pools have a paradoxical dark clarity to them. The water is without sediment and nearly without riffle; ladled into a glass it might seem no different from any other. Yet the deeply mottled light is darker than mere shade, and the pool floors are carpeted in decaying cedar and fir needles.

The first time we entered The Forest Primeval we took our fly rods and fished every one of those little runs and pools. We found that there are trout in The Forest Primeval. They are both tiny (but not immature) and of a beauty unrivaled any place else in the valley. These are not trout to entice the fisher who wants a trophy, nor the searcher for the brightly colored cutthroat of the open water. These are miniature specimen trout, seeming to be almost of a kind of their own. The darkness of the forest, and the even darker bottoms of the pools produce the camouflage into which the trout have evolved. The trout are skittish and wary, and although we caught a few we saw many more dart away under a log or a ledge. If The Forest Primeval is different from the other woods I walk, the trout primeval are just as unique.

The Forest Primeval does not extend more than a half-mile or so up the creek, perhaps not even that far. In my mind, though, it could cover the globe. It has a mystique that suggests that one could wander up the forest into a hidden region that has no known or familiar dimension; that somewhere in here would be the sacred, sheltered opening into the nether world—below the surface, or beyond the creek or under one of the pools.

In fact, though, for me The Forest Primeval does contain that entry point into another world, no less real but far less concrete than the one from which I come. My mind travels far faster than my feet when in that forest, and my mind can make that trip even when my body cannot. I sometimes sit at home and place my emotions and my imagination in the forest. The mystery and the faded veil remain, but the effect is as sharp in memory as in the actual visit.

When I want to return to the place that is the origin, that is essential, the place where I think God would be if I could make mind and matter reduce the unknowable, in my mind at least I go to The Forest Primeval. It is not the place of brightly lit heavens, nor of the inferno hell, nor even of the neutral rest. It is a place like a dusk at dawn. The closest I can come to a parallel image is the feeling I had after Mt. St. Helens erupted. It was a bright Sunday afternoon and we were at a church picnic. This long, low, charcoal-colored, cigar-shaped cloud appeared on the western horizon. We first mistook it for an oncoming storm. It was too uniform, though, too steady in its movement, too inexorable in its progress across the sky. As the ash came on, the sun sank lower in the opposite direction, as if they were on a path to war. Then the sun fell behind the ash cloud, with the light looping over the top. The cloud, never giving the ground already captured, passed over and moved to the east beyond us, but the curved light from the far west still circled around and actually passed over the cloud, and the residue of light seemed to filter faintly back to us from the east as if it were a late afternoon dawn. But it wasn't right, it wasn't natural, it was of a different set of dimensions and rules. The oncoming darkness gave pause, and forced consideration of personal fundamentals, of how we have lived and how we want. In that way so does The Forest Primeval seem to capture my soul.

The Forest Primeval is a place to which I seldom return, either in fact or in mind. It leads me to places I often am not comfortable going, for I must confront who I am and what makes me that way. The answers are not always what I want to know about myself nor what I want others to know. And, The Forest Primeval remains as a reminder of what I cannot, and perhaps should not, know.

Then there is The Meadow. A place or time is defined primarily by the overwhelming presence of something unique or special. When we come to Jeru Creek we travel up the valley carved out by the Pack River from which it derives its name. The surrounding hills are covered by the remnant pine, fir, cedar, and larch forests. In any panorama the sweep of the green crowds out detail save for the silvery band of the running river, and the fall season yellow of tamarack, birch, and aspen. The same is true of the track that leads from the Pack River road back up through the woods to our Jeru Creek cabin. The trees are overwhelming, towering over our drives, and our walks, and our sitting, exaggerated by their tilting posture on the steep hillside above us. The forest provides shelter and shade, but it also clouds the view and creates a false shadow of the premature dusk.

In the foreground of the dominating green of the forest we found The Meadow, an acre of grass, wildflowers, and strawberries that is marked more by our memories and by its contrast to its surroundings than by its special beauty. The Meadow is horizontal in contrast to the vertical face of the mountains and the trees. The Meadow is just off the Pack River road as the car turns sharply to the left, through the gate and back into the woods. The sandy road runs around the perimeter of The Meadow, skirting the edge of the woods, taking nearly three-quarters of a circle before it sharply turns left again and arcs up-ward onto the tree-covered hillside. Once beyond the locked guardian chain, The Meadow always is the first greeting to us as we arrive at the cabin, although the cabin still is another quarter mile away. We enter The Meadow cautiously, hoping for the occasional cow moose with calves, or the white tail deer, or the small bear. The Meadow also carries memories for us that mark its special place.

The Meadow is not, we are told, a natural place. Rather, in the great Sun Dance fire of the 1960s the Forest Service needed a place to land helicopters and to camp its firefighters. So, it cleared out The Meadow. To this day, if one knows where to look, the remnants of the firefighter's camp can still be found.

The Meadow is where our most memorable cabin photo-graph was taken. The picture occurred when Forrest and Lamar were about five and three, two little tow-headed blondes. We were visited by our friends the Spencers with their three children, span-ning the same ages as our own two, one Korean, one Native American, and one African American. In the photograph The Meadow is covered with yellow flowers, many of the plants two and a half or three feet tall. The children hid among the flowers, with their heads barely protruding over the tops. The children added their own bouquet of innocence and delight to The Meadow. Our blondes blended in with the yellow of the flowers, but in turn stood out against the green backdrop of the pines on the perimeter. The darker skins of Nate, Jenny, and Mari, though, contrasted starkly with the foreground, standing out against the paleness of the meadow.

The Spencer and Pierce children at The Meadow

The Spencer children and their parents were our neighbors back home in Pullman. Some fifteen years later, Mari was the first of the five to have a child, making David and Kathy grandparents before us. Jenny and Forrest went through school together, more like cousins than friends, there when needed and irretrievably bound because of the families' shared experiences. When in high school, they went to Mexico together with the rest of the church youth group and cared for young children in the orphanages of Acapulco. Lamar and Nate went through school in the same grades as well. Their interests diverged, as did their social contacts, although like Forrest and Jenny they are bound by our families' shared past in a way over which they have no control. In high school, Lamar was tall and blond, and an effective and methodical basketball player. Nate, a little under six foot, was a state championship level competitor in track and also a basketball player noted by his quickness.

The families remained friends as the children grew older, but during that growth we spent less and less time together. The building of careers, the nurturing of children, the divergence of interests all served to weaken the day-to-day connections, although I think we each knew that, like family, if we showed up they would have to take us in. David and I played city league basketball, golf, and softball together, and for several summers I used his big garden space as a place to recall the ritual growing of corn, squash, and potatoes of my youth. Kathy played the organ in church and Ardith and David sang in the choir while I sat in the congregation wishing I had the talent or the nerve to join them.

Kathy recently became increasingly short of breath, and there was some sense that her lungs no longer were working right. But it wasn't her lungs, it was her heart. She had a tumor growing inside her heart, dangling down into the valve opening between the chambers. The tumor was soft enough that it could break off at any time, enter the bloodstream, and cause a stroke. The tumor showed up on some test I do not understand, and within two days she was in the hospital for open heart surgery. Ardith was there in Spokane right after the operation and talked with Kathy. That night when David came home I met him at his house. Kathy was home herself in a couple of days. And a week later we went to their place for dinner. The dinner was short, but we hoped both a symbolic and a real return to The Meadow of an earlier time.

I know that the good old days were never as good as we imagine, and that even if they were we cannot return there. In many ways I am glad that the road goes only one way. The children of both families now are adults, and ones that continue to enrich our lives. Occasionally, when I see one of them, I am reminded of The Meadow and that long ago time when innocence and nature bound them to each other, to us, and to the shared experiences that have defined our later lives.

§

No place near the cabin is more central to our lives, or carries a more generic name than The Falls. The creek that tumbles and pools directly below the cabin is one of the few in the river valley that stays productive through even the driest summers. It has a short-lived run from the peaks to the west down to the river, perhaps no more than three or four miles, while falling several thousand feet. It seems an unspectacular stream, even though it has played a central symbolic and emotional role in our family for several decades. But there is a very special place on the creek, a place that can be seen from only three vantage points. The first view is from close up, after a walk of a half-hour to forty-five minutes from the cabin. The second place is from the other side of the river valley, high up on the mountain side, looking back to the west. The third is in the guide books to the falls of the Northwest, or those of north Idaho. This place is Jeru Creek Falls, a two-step cascade of some one hundred feet that tumbles over a granite rock face into a deep pool at the bottom. We didn't name "The Falls" but we have trekked to them often.

We leave for The Falls from the cabin and either immediately cross the creek on a fallen tree, or head up our side of the stream for a ways and then cross. If we go up our side, we usually cross just above "Forrest's Hole." Forrest's Hole is a deep pool, at least deep for this small creek, sheltered by large pine and fir, bounded by big boulders, bottomed by a silvery sand, and headed by a small falls. This is where I took Forrest early in the first years of our ownership of Lagniappe. Fishing with a small worm, we always knew we could catch a couple of cutthroat that he could return to the water. And, early in the season—around Memorial Day—we could occasionally hook one of the large spawners, sometimes eighteen to twenty inches long, that stopped to breed in the sandy bottom. This is where Forrest learned to fish, to catch and to release, and because of that it remains a special spot. It has changed, though.

A roughed out clearing for a cabin now rises above the other side, and for a time a white pcv pipe jutted into the underbrush. The path worn there by other young families, who may have attached their own name to the pool, suggests that the fishing no longer is ours alone. Recent spring floods altered the pool physically. The high water washed out the big rocks that headed the pool and created a small falls up which the spawners needed to jump. The pool doesn't look the same, and Forrest rarely fishes there any more. Sometimes when I am at the cabin by myself, though, I will take my fly rod, wander up the forest track, tiptoe up to Forrest's Hole, and try to entice one of the five-inch wonders that still prowl the silica-strewn bed. The point, of course, is not to catch the trout, but to capture the memory of why the place is special and what it was like when Forrest was young.

Neil's Hole is also on the way to The Falls. It is another hundred yards up the creek from Forrest's Hole. We call it Neil's Hole because that's where he caught "Old Man Jeru," our own construction of a legendary mammoth native cutthroat trout that inhabits the creek. Neil's Hole is fairly long for the creek—about twenty-five feet—and quite narrow. At the upper end of the hole two old logs stretch across the creek between the banks. The banks themselves are eight or ten feet above the water, so to fish the hole from the upper end one has to slide down to a resting spot on the logs. The pool there is a corridor between the banks and large rocks. The path that runs along the pool is narrow, sloping toward the water at a sharp angle. There is an old rotten stump that provides some purchase for the walker, but the chance remains that at some point the stump will finally fall away along with one of us. Just beyond the stump and right above the butt-sliding entrance to the top of the hole is a four or five foot crevasse we must leap to continue to The Falls.

We usually approach Neil's Hole from the bottom, as if we were on the way to The Falls, casting a fly backhanded up the stream into the hole's lower reaches. It is impossible to get a free cast into the pool from below without wading out into the little stream and frightening the trout. We usually catch a couple of small cutthroat with the early entreaties. The spawning cutthroat that sometimes are in the pool and the resident cutthroat of any size, though, can be reached only from the top of the hole.

The biggest resident cutthroat caught in the stream—caught and returned many times—emerged out of Neil's Hole, for my brother-in-law Neil was the first one to catch him and he gave him his name—"Old Man Jeru." OMJ probably was female, but that made no difference to our sons who would sneak up on the hole hoping to entice him/her. I don't recall whether OMJ ever was reduced to the creel, but I do know that she is not there any more and the increase in the number of cabins along the creek probably ensures that she never will be. But no matter whether Old Man Jeru is there, or whether Neil's Hole changes with time, which it has, it still will be Neil's Hole because it marks a special place at a special time.

The Forest Primeval is a dark, foreboding place, The Meadow is an emotional place, and Neil's Hole is associated with family ties. The Falls, though, are the mystical terminus of Jeru Creek. About a mile up the creek, beyond the Minnow Ponds, beyond Frog Hollow, and beyond Traveler's Rest—all places on the trek to The Falls that were named by Forrest and Lamar—is a fairy land. This little creek, which in the summer a child can crawl across, year round cascades over an eighty foot falls, after having experimented in a smaller, twenty foot drop directly above. The Falls, as written up in guides to waterfalls or to interesting hikes in northern Idaho, is always characterized as spectacular.

The Falls tumbles out of a horseshoe home high above the pool at the bottom. The smoothed granite surface provides a slide for the water, moving it around the forty foot log that has been caught in the main drop for as long as we have been there. The pool at the bottom is surrounded on three sides by deep ferns, cedar, and Devil's Club, and it too has an aged log angled through the upper end. But it is not the length of the drop, or the size of the pools, or the logs in them that give The Falls its mystical quality. That quality comes from the mist and the miniature worlds that grow in the cracks of the granite wall and are nourished by the tiny droplets of water hanging in the air. Turning the last corner of the path opens up rainbow after rainbow as the light slices through the suspended water canopy. Underneath the waterfall, about half way down, in wedge-shaped enclaves, sits a series of tiny botanical wonderlands. These spaces in the mist-draped rock wall are no bigger than a camp cooler, but sand—undisturbed save for the raking of little ants—tiny ferns, midget grasses, bell flowers two inches high, rivulets of newly condensed creek water on its passage from fall, to mist, to fall again—combine to make a garden more perfect and abstract than human hands can craft.

We do not make the trek to The Falls very often anymore. Years of rough winters have made the trail less passable, and as we, too, age we enjoy more the contemplative respite of the campfire or of the water sound. But, regardless of how often we go or come, we don't really leave The Falls, we just kind of drift away, tailing off down the path as we encroach on the outer boundaries of the water cloud. Back at the cabin, forty-five minutes later, the mystical aura is gone, but a kind of peace reminiscent of the undisturbed world we left re-emerges every time we summon memories of The Falls.

The sanctity of The Forest Primeval, the emotion of The Meadow, the mysticism of The Falls—they provide the soul to our life at the cabin. The simple beauty of Jeru Creek is a wonder. But that beauty is no more than that of any other place until we lay over it the meaning held in what we have named. It is in that naming and what it represents that I recall the depth of what I have gained from being there.

13

The Bogachiel Sonata

Now the sea, now the river
Winds a night watch through
Grottos of pine, windswept and twisted
Straight, gripped, straight like
Sodden green epileptics.
The Bogachiel twists over
Rocks that look like dinner rolls,
Moving through clearcuts,
Raking beaches, briny with
Tracks of seagulls and
Salmon roe. Salmon rows
Huddle like red bullets
In the shaft of the deep current,
Logs of shot ballasting the river's
Keel. It drifts,
Half-sail, toward
The Pacific….
I said take me fishing
You drove me in your white
International along slick
Corkscrew roads through
Stubble, clear cuts and
Wind wracked pine. I said
Where are we going you said
Upstream.
There were no seat belts.
As we dove left then
Right through green frothy
Hallways bits of river
Flashed in the woods like
Subway windows.

Later, the memory
Of your backwoods eyes
Explained to me how the
River works, how tides
Shirk salt into the forest's toes,
How roads flow like
Rivers at corners.
I can see a hill gripping
Truck and girl, slithery;
They grow smooth with the years
Like broken glass as it
Washes them, pleading,
Seaward.
—Forrest Pierce, 1994

"Hey, Dad!" my blonde, gangly, six-foot-four-inch, fifteen-year-old son Forrest called out, interrupting my late summer reverie. We were slowly descending from a laconic, generally half-hearted fishing foray that had taken us from the cabin and up the narrow trail along the side of the serpentine, cedar and fir shaded, fern bordered Jeru Creek. We had just been to The Falls. It was late in the afternoon on a mid-August Sunday, the temperature in the low 90s and the humidity feeling somewhere in the same vicinity, an unusual combination in the ordinarily cool, shaded mountains of north Idaho.

That particular day we had not wasted much effort in serious fishing. In fact, rarely do we practice the angler's art with much rigor anymore, at least when we go on an excursion up Jeru Creek. The serious fishing on that little stream is long gone, resting somewhere in our memories.

After the twenty years that we have been frequent visitors to the creek, all that now remains of the angler's quarry are the tiny remnants of a fertile resident cutthroat fishery that even in the

good old days produced only ten-inch giants at best. The increasing pressure of more cabins on the creek, and their inhabitants' unwillingness to protect the jewel they view there, have erased any pretence we once had of again living out one of those fishing days that produce the boasting stories of success told around family fires.

So, these days when we take one of our rare journeys up Jeru Creek toward the crystalline, soul-restoring falls, we do so for less instrumental reasons, at least less instrumental to those goals we used to pursue that are connected with the catching of fish. Instead, anymore I think we really are trying to reach out emotionally, and at least partially renourish our memories of those early days. We also find the trek to The Falls to be a meditative venture. At least when Forrest and I go together, we spread ourselves apart some, barely staying in each other's sight as we meander along the trail, or as we duck alone down to some hidden pool on the creek. And as we return down the trail to the cabin our thoughts wander as well.

Jeru Creek and the falls that interrupt it lend themselves to silence and to solitude. And silence is a common state when Forrest and I are together. We do talk to each other quite a bit, but it usually is pretty focused stuff. We do not engage in the casual chatter that accompanies many of the larger family walks in the woods. When Forrest and I go on long car trips together, each other's company usually seems to be sufficient, and there is little need to make random observations about what we see, or what we are thinking. Since he was a toddler, others have said that they observe a special non-verbal kind of communication between us. If so, that connection may come from our having spent so much time together, as is wont for a father with his first born son, before the attention is divided with a brother. And our unseen sense of each other may be remnant from my first wondrous sighting of him, our eyes seeming to lock in the New Orleans hospital as he was wheeled out from the birthing room, beat-up and bruised from the use of forceps to turn him in his mother's womb. Or, it may just be that we simply feel the same way, and so our responses to the same situation are inadvertently congruous.

So, it should be no surprise that my parental response to Forrest's call was without much energy. "What, son?" I countered, in my rather sardonic and perhaps slightly disinterested way. I did not know what startling adolescent query the Jeru Creek walk might have made ready to confront my unprepared fatherhood; I was off in my own private world.

Undeterred by my preoccupied, distant answer, Forrest continued, "Dad, when you walk around up here, do you hear music in your head?"

After a brief pause, searching for something reasonable and supportive to say, and not wanting to reveal my instant concern about a child who has just confessed to hearing things, I decided to play it safe.

"No, son, I don't," I said as calmly as I could muster. "Why do you ask?"

In his diffident, teenage style, Forrest continued, "Oh, nothing . . . it's just that when I am out here, there is this music that keeps popping up inside me, and I wondered if that happens to you, too."

"No, it doesn't, son," I readily confessed. "So, what kind of music do you hear? Elton John, or Sting, or the Police?"

"No, Dad! I don't hear anybody else's music. I hear my own music, but I haven't written it yet. It's just there, inside me."

"Well, son," I closed off the conversation as gently as I could, "I'm sorry, but there's not a lot I can help you with on this one."

That incident happened years ago, but I was reminded of it very recently while around a cook fire, in the Absoroka Mountains of Wyoming. We were above 10,000 feet in elevation, straddling the high continental divide, looking off toward Yellowstone in one direction and the Grand Tetons in the other. Ardith and I were near the end of an eight-day horse-pack trip we had taken with our good friends from Jackson Hole, Leigh and Marilyn Stowell, their two daughters Erica and Stephanie, and Marilyn's sister Nancy and her husband Tom from Chicago.

We were guided by two unusual outfitter brothers, Pike and Press Stephens. Press's Faraway Ranch is near Dubois (pronounced doo-boys) Wyoming. Pike holds a Ph.D. in chemistry, teaching at a college in Puerto Rico. He comes to Wyoming each summer to work with Press in the mountains. Press Stephens himself is a guitar playing, several time "outfitter-of-the-year," who leaves his campsites as nearly undisturbed environmentally as possible. Press's joy in the wonder of the Wyoming high country was perhaps best expressed in the minutes after Stephanie Stowell had spotted a herd of bighorn sheep. We had been looking for sheep for the whole trip and had yet to find any, leaving Press sorely disappointed. On our last day Stephanie's sharp eyes picked up the animals' movements. The sheep were high on another ridge, far across a deep canyon, barely visible to the naked eye except perhaps for those with the far-sighted gift of the young. Every few seconds after that sighting, from his saddle, Press would erupt in spontaneous joy, his arms spread out in affirmation, exulting to us and to the mountains, as he raised up high in his stirrups, shouting "SHEEP! SHEEP! SHEEP!"

On about the fifth day of the trip, in the early evening, Press and I were standing in the cold, mountain rain around the cook fire. The others were under the large canvas fly protecting the food from the elements, aided by the shelter of plastic wrapped wine. I learned that our wrangler from Wyoming held a master's degree in art history from an elite Eastern school. I asked him what his thesis had been about, frankly expecting something uninspiring, perhaps even having to do with the ever present Western wildlife art of the local area. Indeed, it would not have surprised me if his thesis title had been "SHEEP!"

Instead, Press told me that his thesis compared Winslow Homer to another landscape artist, Rockwell Kent, who had done a lot of painting in Alaska. Press contrasted Homer and Kent in terms of the relationship of their art to their personal connection to nature. As I reconstruct it now, albeit at a much lower altitude, and free from the plastic encased wine, Press said that he had argued that Winslow Homer applied his art to nature, but that Rockwell Kent expressed his sense of nature in his art. For Homer, according to Press, nature was the vehicle for his love of art; for Kent, though, art was the vehicle for his love of nature.

Now, years after that late summer walk up Jeru Creek, Forrest is a composer who still has music filling up his head. That music expresses his synthesis with rivers and mountains and the creatures that inhabit them. I think the rivers and hills he composes about are the vehicle for the music in his head, but they also are the source of it. So, Press's words about the painters Homer and Kent inevitably drew me to reflect on Forrest's development as an artist—mostly as composer, but also as poet—and on those rivers and mountains that emerge as the precursor models of those sounds in his head. I also saw clearly how that inseparable intermingling of Forrest's life and his music has defined who he is, and how our own relationship has been entangled in music and in rivers.

There is a lot to think about with regard to one's child, and like all people Forrest is complex and multi-dimensional, and his complexity surely also shaped how I evolved as a father. Perhaps a brief biography of Forrest would provide the context for what follows. He was born in New Orleans in July 1972, on a classic hot southern stormy night. It was a very difficult birth for his mother. She probably would not have survived, the doctors said, had she not been in the hospital.

Forrest began playing the piano when he was five, and started composing at the age of eight. He continued to compose and study piano through his high school years, mixing music with sports and studies. Always tall for his age, six-foot-six-inches by the time he was seventeen, he was naturally drawn to basketball. He and his friends played in the seventh grade national Junior Olympic Championships in Iowa City, and as high school seniors they placed near the top of the state tournament. Their early basketball magic was a gift of opportunity and delight to them and their parents, and a constant pressure on them to succeed beyond what any of them really wanted or needed themselves.

Forrest's first composition, a short piece for piano titled "My Dad," was entered in the local PTSA Reflections contest when he was in the third grade. "My Dad" went on to win first prize for the state and then honorable mention at the national level. From then on, he continued to write music, although on the surface it never seemed to capture him entirely. Until late in his teens, Forrest would write only one or two pieces each year, usually under the deadline constraint of a competition his piano teachers would encourage him to enter.

Forrest studied music at the University of Puget Sound, took his master's in composition at Minnesota, and went on to a doctoral program in composition at Indiana University. But he still plays basketball in the gym on the weekend, and when I go to visit him and it's not too cold outside, we make a very slow ritual dance around the hoop as I try to maintain some semblance of the hereditary link between his art and my age.

Forrest is married to Jaci, a dancer, writer, and wonderful friend of his and ours. They provide love and grace to each other in the tough times they both have. Late this summer a doctor told Forrest that a biopsy, taken after some abnormal bleeding, showed that he has Chron's disease, an often genetically transmitted, autoimmune system produced, ulcerative invasion of the intestines. We are told that the seriousness of Chron's disease varies widely among people who suffer from it, and that his might not be so bad. But then an arthritic-like condition erupted in his right wrist and hand, itself sometimes a symptom of Chron's. This prohibits him from practicing the piano. This discovery of the Chron's disease the week after our mountain trip sobered considerably my later reflections about the Absoroka campfire, even as it now forces me to carefully peel back the layers of my relationship to this first born who has produced so much wonder in my life.

Forrest started playing the piano about the same time he started fishing in Jeru Creek, and about the same time he started trying to propel a round ball up toward a hoop. I taught him how to shoot the basketball and how to fish for the trout, and I sat with him every evening after dinner while he practiced the piano. The hoops, the trout, and the music both blessed our connections and strained our bonds. The fishing and the basketball were partly mine, but the music was all his. I sat, walked, and ran with this child, whose life seemed to promise the return of so much in so many ways, if I were the right kind of father. So much of that promise has been kept, but in retrospect I know that the burden Forrest feels about what he needs to achieve cannot be unlinked from my own investment and interference in his life. I cannot know who Forrest would be if I had parented differently, and less intensively. Perhaps there is some arrogance in believing that a parent really makes a difference. Some parts of what he does surely would have a different shape, but the music would have been there anyway, floating around inside his head. But I also must know that the emotional pain he often feels, the sorrow he sometimes carries, and his need for affirmation, also are very much my burden to carry.

At five, Forrest developed a friendship with Cliff, a boy across the street whose mother was a pianist. At his request, Mrs. Watson agreed to teach Forrest some basic music on the piano. Ardith and I both were intrigued by this interest of his. I had played the piano, but did not start lessons until I was in the seventh grade. At the encouragement of a teacher, I stopped after my first semester of college piano. Ardith took lessons when she was young, but her forte was singing, and she was a voice minor in college. A gift for music seemed a mystery to me, but Cliff's mother thought Forrest might have it. So, Forrest soon moved to formal lessons, with a different teacher. Every night after dinner, at least for the first few years, he and I would go downstairs to the "green room" (so named because of the color of the rug), where we had placed the piano on which his mother and her mother both had learned to play. We would sit at the piano bench while he went through his weekly lesson material. At least as I recall it, it was a pleasant experience, a time where we knew we could be together each day. I am sure that on occasion I was too directive, but I have no recollection of an authoritarian role, for Forrest progressed rapidly without my assistance, and he never asked to be released from the routine. I simply enjoyed being there with him, and giving some advice where I could.

It also was about the age of five when I first introduced Forrest to trout fishing on Jeru Creek. Late in the summer, when the stream was low, the young cutthroat were learning to feed with no timidity, and the sun too was low in the day, we would take the cedar shake steps down from the cabin to the stream. We then would follow the path along the stream, moving slowly up the creek. We carried along a short fiberglass spinning rod and an open-faced reel; the line terminated in a number ten or twelve worm hook. The little piece of night crawler we threaded on the hook became the entry point to Forrest's fishing world. We would dip the hook and its dismembered passenger in each of the small, clear pools and riffles as we moved up the stream. We were sure to catch a half dozen or so small, red-bellied, slash-throated trout along the way. But the final destination of the trip was a pool just at the upper end of our stretch of the stream. It was this special spot that we christened Forrest's Hole.

Forrest and Lamar at Jeru Creek

Forrest's Hole was a place where the innocent fisher child could naively bask in the perfection of the natural world. We approached this special water from the shaded side, carefully snaking our way along a narrow, bare log before we ducked through fruit-laden huckleberry bushes. We poised the rod over the bank's edge and swung the piece of worm out to where it could drop into the upper reaches of the water. Up from the bottom would dart trout after trout, attacking cast after cast, until we had exhausted the stream's larder or our interest. Rarely did we keep a trout from Forrest's Hole, aiming to preserve the magic there.

Those tiny, late summer cutthroat provided that magic, but not the angling drama in Forrest's Hole. The drama came in the spring when the season first opened and the unabated snow melt rushed madly through the normally protected water, moving around and over the rocks and the logs that framed it. It was the spring flood that also harbored the mature, spawning cutthroat that made their way up the Pack River from Lake Pend Oreille, replenishing their kind on the gravelly, sandy bottom of Jeru Creek's Forrest's Hole. Forrest and I occasionally would catch one of the spawners, the distorted, brightly hued and misshapen adult cutthroat stretching nearly two feet long. We returned them to the stream.

Forrest is the "purist" of the fishermen in our family, perhaps growing out of the early reverence of the hole named for him. While his younger brother Lamar and I love the sanctuary-like wonder of the creek and the river, we go there to catch fish as well. Forrest, though, seems to worship there. And, I know that deep down he aches every time he pulls a cutthroat from the water. He bends down the barbs on the hook, and when he catches one he stands reverently over the soon to be released trout, holding it gently in his long, graceful, ivory-stroking fingers, washing the red-streaked gills in the river's life-restoring liquid. And obvious anguish fills his face when the trout succumbs to the trauma of its capture. The moral weight he carries with the life and death of the fish is not always easy for me to manage, and it causes me to think twice about the freedom with which I more cavalierly treat the trout. In his love of the stream and its contents, Forrest has become what I admire, and now I wonder at its cost to him. He believes deeply and strongly, and without compromise, about the actions of others to be sure, but even more about his own and their consequences for other living things. And it is the self-reflective, silent, contemplative judgment of his own behavior and its meaning that weighs on him. But it also is the place where his music finds its origins—in the cerebral and emotional garden where guilt, conscience, empathy, hope, and a firm belief in what is good all merge with nature to husband his aesthetic.

I both admire and trouble at the musical produce of that joining of spirit and mind. His creations are moving to me and central to my life. Often, late in the office day, after others have left and gone home, and I search for the connections that mean the most to me, I listen to CDs or tapes of Forrest's work. "The House of David," "My Dad" and "Rhododendron" comfort me when I need solace. But his clarity of vision of what is right and where he falls short mirrors my own weakness there. Seeing it in him, and in the pain it sometimes causes, forces me to confront my own weakness and my own inability to provide him the insight while protecting him from the ache.

Our shared entanglement with the emotion-producing wonder of Jeru Creek explains much of what has linked me so closely with Forrest. Lamar and I deeply love each other, and we engage intimately on an intellectual level—partly because we consciously are afraid of where emotional combat will lead us. Forrest and I seem to have another kind of connection. In a sense, where Lamar and I think alike, Forrest and I seem to feel alike. There is a fundamental sense of sharing something unspoken and perhaps unspeakable. When we fish, or when we travel, or walk, or sit together in front of the television watching college basketball there seems an assumed communication. It is not unusual for husbands and wives, after years of marriage, to be able to finish out each other's thoughts and emotions. But since he was a young teenager, if I paused or searched for the completion of a thought, Forrest could do it for me.

The Bogachiel River sits on the western slope of the Olympic Mountains. It has a relatively short course to the sea, and passes into the salt water not far from the town of Forks. I first entered the Bogachiel as a college student, visiting my friends Al and Betty Kitchel, who grew up there. We used their riverside home farm as a base for a weekend excursion into the mountains. It was many years later that we returned to the Bogachiel, this time with our family to spend another few days with Al and Betty. We stayed in a small cabin that Al had built on the farmland, a stone's throw from the Bogachiel River's banks.

Near the end of our stay at Forks, the Kitchels' niece Melanie—who lived on the farm—met up with Forrest. She was a year or two younger than Forrest, bright, attractive, talented athletically and personally. She took Forrest, and Lamar as I recall, on an evening fishing trip somewhere up the river. They left in the pickup and came back after dark, only a few hours later. They caught no fish, but had a great time, and there seemed to develop a connection between them with some promise for a long-term friendship.

Out of that stay developed Forrest's first major piano composition, The Bogachiel Sonata, a page from which is at the front of this chapter. The Bogachiel Sonata won prizes for him, including the regional collegiate composition competition, while he still was in high school. The local ballet company choreographed a dance to that work, and later he returned to Pullman to play the piano in accompaniment to the dance in a public performance. Immediately after the dance performance I ran into the Washington State University basketball coach, Kelvin Sampson, for whom Forrest had played for years in the summer basketball camp. He and Forrest had become quite good friends, and Kelvin had encouraged him—in a very realistic way—to continue to play basketball for a small college some place, and to devote more time to preparing for that. There were no false expectations, but I think there was a kind of puzzlement as to why this tall, graceful young man with some athletic potential did not take the sport more seriously. Kelvin was at the ballet performance to see his own daughter dance in another piece. After the performance, Kelvin came up to me and simply said "That was wonderful, John. Now, I understand."

The Bogachiel Sonata that produced the ballet expressed the music in Forrest and the connection he felt with the river. But, the Bogachiel also had a tragic side that I know lodged painfully in Forrest. The next spring after the family visit to the cabin, Melanie was driving the same pickup to school. Olympic rain forest weather had returned. In the dark mist of the early morning, the ancient truck skidded off the road, and with no seatbelt, that talented, lovely young woman was killed. When we told Forrest about her death, there was his characteristic retreat into silence at the sadness. But we should have known that the mourning had deeply rooted at the place where his music and his art also rest. Out of that unseen source came the Bogachiel Sonata, as well as the poem at the beginning of this essay, which recalls Melanie's death.

A couple of summers ago, I watched this same tall, now elegant young man walk out on the stage at the Aspen Music Festival to introduce a composition for a quintet that he had written called "Rhododendron." In the audience were other members of this select, senior master class in composition, along with several Pulitzer Prize winning composers, people from Aspen indulging in the arts, and assorted family and friends of the composers and performers. This piece of Forrest's came at about the middle of the program, preceded by several works of other participants in the institute. The oral program notes spoken from the stage by the composers had uniformly been technical and theoretical in content: "This piece was written in order to explore the inverted 7th minor matrix in xenophobic pentameter" or something like that.

In a full cycle to that first composition, "My Dad," over fifteen years earlier, Forrest now said to everyone there, "I wrote this music for my father, in memory of his father." Forrest's grandfather had died of a sudden heart attack when I was thirteen. The church youth group of which I was a member had purchased a rhododendron in memory of my father and it was planted next to the entry steps of the church. Some years later, a new church was built, and the rhododendron was moved, along with the hymnals and the pews. The shrub has since rested there, underneath the sheltered edge of the sanctuary. Ever since that painful planting, I have always paid special heed to the rhododendron as a living connection to my past.

When Forrest was in college in Tacoma, occasionally he would drive out to Yelm for church with his grandmother. One Sunday after the service she took him outside the sanctuary and showed him the rhododendron in full bloom, its bouquets of white flowers suffusing the air with their fragrance. Although Forrest briefly mentioned the visit, in later years it was clear that this introduction to a part of his past must have moved him deeply, for he had never known either of his grandfathers. At Aspen, that white rhododendron and the loss it represented surfaced as chamber music, containing in it percussive sounds from milk bottles and wheel drums (my father drove a milk truck), and the haunting adaptation of a Methodist funeral hymn.

The kind of choices and commitment to a life that Forrest had to make surfaced in the spring of his senior year in high school. Forrest had applied to a handful of small liberal arts schools, including some in the Midwest. His applications were governed by three factors—the academic reputation of the schools, their interest in his basketball playing, and the presence of a school of music that could respond to his desire to prepare himself for a possible profession. Forrest had not yet decided which direction he wanted to push his life. One of the schools was strongly recruiting him for basketball, but did not have the resources to support the kind of music he wanted to learn to write. Another school had a very strong interest in his music but did not show much interest in his jump shot. Both schools were prepared to provide him with some scholarship support.

One Sunday night in May, Forrest received two phone calls in close proximity to each other. The first was from the school of music in which he was interested. That was followed shortly by one from the basketball coach from the other school. Forrest took the calls on the portable phone in the living room. I stayed in the family room and intentionally tried not to make him feel uncomfortable at this difficult time. I think at one level I hoped that he could have both—he could play basketball now, and do his music later, or maybe do them together, for if he didn't play basketball now he never would have the same chance again, at least to formally represent a college. That tilt toward sports probably reflected my own aborted aspirations of nearly thirty years earlier. I had been a small town basketball star and had dreams of playing at a higher level. I was a "walk-on" at college and played a couple of years of junior varsity basketball, traveling to community colleges and penitentiaries in the Puget Sound area.

Even though I had this secret hope that Forrest would play basketball, partly to fulfill my dreams, I was even prouder that he had a choice. And I knew I would be proud when he made his own decision. So, after he had hung up from his conversation with the basketball coach, he came into the family room. I stood up and walked over to him, asking him what he had done. He said that he had just told the coach that he was not going to his school to play basketball, but that he had decided to devote his education to music. I said to him, "O.K. son, that's fine with me." Through tears, though, he said to me, "But, Dad, I always wanted to be better than you." I said to him, "Son, you already are." He already was better than I was in his music, to no one's doubt, and he was better than I was in basketball, although he couldn't prove it yet. But he also was better than me in that he had the choice of which one he would do, and he made the right choice and one I probably would not have made at his age.

Forrest had the strength to make the choice that showed who he really was, rather than who he wanted others to think he was, or who they wanted him to be, including me. In that family room Forrest told me in a different way the same thing that he had told me on that walk back from Jeru Creek—he could still hear the music inside him, and it was louder and more powerful than any approbation he might hear on the hardwood, or in his father's voice.

14

Violation

I N THE OUTDOORS, "violation" conjures up the image of some slob-like jerk flailing about on a pristine stream. I suppose that such an ordinary, bad-sporting sense of the word is part of what I mean. Catching too many fish, or catching them at the wrong time of the year, or with the wrong methods—these all surely are violations of the fish and game laws and of the sensibilities of those who care about them. But that is not my only mental picture of the meaning of violation.

It is true that in the nearly twenty years that we have wandered up and down the Pack River and its tributaries, my family and I have seen very little of the fishing pigs depicted in the most degrading caricatures of outdoor life. And only once have I been checked by a fish and game official hunting for evidence of this ordinary kind of violation. It was a couple of summers ago that Lamar and I were coming back from an afternoon trek up one of the Pack River's feeder streams. We had a glorious afternoon, catching dozens of small cutthroat on Renegades and Yellow Humpies, releasing them all. We had no need, nor even an urge, to keep the fish. Neither one of us is ideologically opposed to keeping some fish to eat, although we rarely do. It was just that it was a mellow day, one in which death, even if of a small fish, filled no pressing need for us. In a way, I guess the killing of the fish itself would have seemed a violation of the mood.

So we were surprised, and perhaps even a little disconcerted, to be stopped at the Pack River bridge by two of Idaho's fish and game wardens. The bridge is a couple of miles up the road from Jeru Creek, the location of our cabin, and symbolically marks the point where relatively casual travel on the river road ends (or begins, when returning). Above the bridge, the road is barely maintained, each year becoming more difficult to pass. There is even a suspicion among locals that the Forest Service intends to abandon that portion of the road sometime soon, after the latest round of logging has been concluded. Unlike the eight miles of washboard county road that precedes it, the five miles of Forest Service road up to the bridge is narrow and graded, with gravel overlain with some kind of adhesive to create a base to support the logging trucks. Above the bridge the rutted course is more like the corrugated wood roads of old, only without the wood. So the return down the road to the bridge and to the officers waiting on the other side was a re-entry into the world of not only smooth roads, but also of regulation and enforcement.

The first warden came up to our red painted pickup, stuck his head in the window, and asked in a friendly way if we had been fishing. In a similarly amiable response, we affirmed that indeed we had been fishing. Then the official's companion asked more gruffly (good guy, bad guy, I guess) to examine our licenses and inquired as to whether we had caught any fish. We allowed as how, yes, we had caught fish and quite a few of them but had not kept any.

Along with an old canvas creel, our beat-up graphite fly rods had been thrown in the back of the pickup. The officers prowled around the outside, peering into the cab and around the bed. It was clear that the green-jacketed sleuths were hunting for a hidden violation, perhaps in a telltale bulge in the creel or in a protruding tail or a worm hook on the line (the latter signaling the unlikelihood of our purist claim of returning the fish to the stream).

We presumed the violation for which the wardens searched was fish related, linked to our blithely claimed success, but it was not clear where they thought we could have stashed the fish we denied having. There was no search of the wheel well, at least that we could see from the cab, or under the seats in the front. But the scrutiny was intense. In retrospect, though, given our scruffy exteriors (we had been at the cabin for several days), the character of the Pack River Valley and both its visitors and its residents, some other stash may have been the target.

Indeed, the illegal crops grown in the logged hills of north Idaho, and smoked in many other locations, are legendary both for their quality and their quantity. The hemp horticulture of the forest does lead to considerable caution in our treks up the creeks, lest we disturb the guardians of the crops. I do not know if officials are ever successful in their search for the grass-growing quarry. This time, though, the officers came up empty—no fish, no grass, no illegal firearms. At that time, in my mind, the only violation was theirs. No doubt doing their job with integrity and efficiency, they nonetheless had tainted what had been a special day. So, the remainder of our trip down the road was less light-hearted, less lost in the bright success we had enjoyed on the stream and the comfort in each other's company.

But none of these—the ordinary fishing infraction, the mood breaker, or the mood alterer—is the kind of violation I have in mind. The violation of which I write is centered more in the rupture of fundamental relationships, both personal and natural. This other kind of violation reflects damage to the most elemental reasons we have for being on Jeru Creek and the Pack River.

The trek to the river surely invokes different motives for different people. Our search for mellowness on a deep summer afternoon was only one of those, and probably not even one of the most significant. For some, including me in my youth, river fishing is a time to prove one's manhood in a contest with the wild. The long drive up a narrow, rutted, gravel road that winds through darkly tunneled evergreens may recall some primitive, partially conquered fear of venturing outside the campfire light. Returning unscathed from the test of the unknown danger, and sometimes with nature's booty in hand or creel, provides a validation for one's belief in his (or her, I presume, although this seems to be a particularly male quirk) capacity to face unafraid the even more foreboding dangers of modern society. Victory is ours!

Going "up the creek," even without the proverbial paddle, also can be a time of constructed escape from the constant travail of daily life. The facade of stillness, quiet, and peace in the natural environment may only vaguely veil the presence of real dangers, some inherent and others imposed, that lurk in the primitive woods. There are grizzly bears and there are militia, although we have seen neither such beast nor such man, at least in their clearly identifiable forms. So, we try to ignore the threat of them both, and see the woods as a place to hide. That retreat to the staged draping of nature's inescapable brutality and pain may even serve to shield also, however temporarily, the damaging malice or the fabricated injury of the "real world." That the eventual return to town means the social wounds will surely reopen serves to dampen, but it does not really eliminate, the emotional soothing that comes from escaping to nature.

The nature trek also is a time of reverence and searching, rather than of concealment. We may not always know the quarry of the hunt, but the frequent longing to find in the unknown something undefined and unfound in the daily world leads to both physical and metaphorical journeys. Whether anything specific is uncovered there in nature seems less important than the belief that there is in fact something to be discovered—an answer, a balm, a comfort that will ease the ache and heal the wound.

No doubt, though, I do all of the above. I am sure that I search, and that I hide, and that I hope to heal as I wander up Jeru, and that the journey continues even as my memory later retraces those treks through the back channels of my mind. But, the reality is that this pantheon of potentially grace-giving gods I pursue up the Pack River does not leave me unscathed, either physically or emotionally.

I have fallen off logs and onto boulders, and I have scratched and poisoned my legs with the toxins of Devil's Club and stinging nettles. My extremities are marred and scarred at the end of each summer, proud symbols of having survived another lunge at recapturing only vaguely recalled youthful capacities. But the physical pain hurts nothing like the violations of the soul and of the senses. There can be an inner pain almost as sharp and as stabbing as the pocket knife, or as abrupt as the awkward tumble from a mountain bike, or as sobering as the catapult off the rain-soaked log into the river or onto its rocks. This other pain comes when I witness the casual and cavalier violation of nature, especially when it intrudes into my own personal world.

In retrospect, such violations of nature may often seem more constructed than real; they probably grow from my personal sensitivities as much as from the malevolent intent of another person or the actual insult to the environment. At the same time, for some people, there seems to exist an implicit fatalism that says that everything that happens is subject to the laws of nature; so, nothing can happen that is a violation of those laws. But what may not seem to be a violation in the minds of others can certainly strike sharply at my own sensibilities.

But, this raises the question: Why do some things violate my sensibilities and others do not? Why is it that hearing a chain saw in the woods doesn't bother me nearly as much as the raucous outburst of a trail bike or a four wheeler following me up one of the local trails? Why are my senses seemingly violated by the reflections of a sun-shattering beer can lodged in a tangle of brush high on the West Branch, far from any road, but not by finding a lost metal fishing lure gleaming in the water just around the bend of the same stream? Why is it that something deep inside me rebels at the thought or the sound of a pack of hunter-led dogs chasing a bear down the river valley, but not at the image of a wolf stalking a deer? Why is it acceptable for my sons and me to catch and release dozens of trout in an afternoon, but I reject with some anger the person who takes home thirty fish with the limit six, because he says he is only going to be able to fish once this month and so he ought to get to keep the limit for all of the other times he would have fished if he could have? Why is it no problem to me for our small cabin to have a pipe in the creek to withdraw bathing water but I feel violated when a quarter-mile-long pipe runs

"This Other Pain," Jo Hockenhull, 1999

down the middle of the river to fill a pond scoured out of the bank with a bulldozer? And, why do I revel in the richness and human diversity of Seattle's growing urban chaos but bristle at the encroachment of even a faint hint of those same civilizing influences in the Pack River Valley?

The sense of violation for me grows not out of a clear contrast between someone's behavior and an accepted explicit ethical standard I hold for what is right or wrong, correct or incorrect, just or unjust. I wish I could rationalize my reactions with such clear reason or tight logic, but those boundaries are just too fuzzy for me.

My sense of violation seems to strike more viscerally, emerging out of discord between the senses and the soul, leaving out the more rational side of my mind. My sense of violation comes from a clash of images, the one in my head that maps a mutually nurturing relationship that stands in conflict with the painfully exploitative picture I often see played out in front of me.

The dissonant image I sometimes see in front of me creates a bright emotional pain, starkly in contrast to the mellow comfort of the relaxed fishing that Lamar and I enjoyed that warm summer day. Only recently, I have tried to understand my encounter with two young people laying a large white pipe directly down the middle of the spawning beds of Jeru Creek. My older son Forrest and I were finishing the outside work on a small addition to the cabin, a shower room that we had enclosed and incorporated into the main part of the dwelling. While we disturbed the chipmunks and the jays with our hammering and my occasional outbursts of thumb-flattened pain, we were making progress, Forrest's work more elegant than mine, but both serviceable. While putting some cedar shakes on the cabin, I saw movement down below us on the stream. The distraction was the white flash of plastic pipe being hurled down the creek.

A young man and a young woman were wading down the center of Jeru, slogging through the runs and the pools where in the spring runoff two-foot long spawners regenerate their kind and where even in the low flow of late summer small cutthroat dart. Almost before I knew it, I ran and stumbled down the steep path to the stream, ending up standing a few feet behind the young man. The noise of the stream had hidden my approach, and he was unaware of my presence. To break through the creek noise, and surely to express my anger, I yelled to the pipe layer, aggressively asking him what he was doing. He jerked in surprise at my intrusion. He said he was laying pipe from the top of our property all of the way down to where the creek crosses the road, a good quarter mile or more below, and if I had any problems with it I could get in touch with his boss. His boss is the seemingly ageless owner of land up and down the valley, said to have been gained through tax sales after the depression.

I indicated with some fervor my disgust and anger at what I saw to be the unthinking action. I told the young people that they could not walk on our property to lay the pipe (we had just bought the other side of the stream in the mistaken belief that it would increase our control over the stream itself). Of course, in my anger the illogic escaped me, for asking them to do the opposite, walking on our property and out of the stream, would have been more protective of the waterway.

The pipe layers continued on their way as I fumed internally while I retreated back to the cabin. The visceral reaction did fade into anger and then eventually into a kind of fatalistic, low-grade disgust. But still I failed to understand why he intentionally would violate Jeru Creek that way. The cabins down the stream did not need the water; there was plenty for the taking at any point in the flow. Besides, if we owned both sides of the stream how could he have passageway for his pipe?

I looked back through our paperwork and through my memory to come up with the answer. The documents showed me that the clever man has platted the lots up to the high water mark of the stream, all of the way down the stream for nearly a half mile. Then, he made the streambed itself another piece of property to which he retained title. Now I do not know whether streams can be owned separately from the land they border, but the map we have has Jeru Creek as a parcel all of its own. That mapping obviously was the foundation for the claim to the streambed over which the water moved with such clarity. But why the pipe? We think the answer is found in the attempt by the State of Idaho to allocate water rights on all streams in the state some years ago. We applied for and received rights for withdrawing water for domestic use for our small group of cabins. Our guess is that he had filed at about the same time or a little earlier at the head of this reach of the stream. But, he had not exercised his rights, and there may be some provision that failure to exercise the rights will result in their loss. So, we figure that the pipe was to preserve the water rights for the potential need for some later time. Legal or not, each time I looked at the glaring white sore I would again feel the hot surge of anger.

The human-centered violation of Jeru has a lingering effect, even though about six weeks after the pipe went in the creek, it came out—or at least most of it came out. Along our stretch of the creek, and for much of the creek below us, the pipe no longer snakes through the pools and riffles. There are a few lengths thrown up in the woods, and one that is still lodged in the creek down a ways. Most of the pipe, though, is roughly stacked in a recently bulldozed clearing across the stream and up a couple of hundred feet from the top of our property. It is not clear whether the long tubes are ready for re-entry into the stream, or for removal. The remnants of the strands that remain near or in the stream, though, suggest that re-entry after the high waters of the winter and spring have abated is to be predicted. But perhaps not; perhaps the water right has been established and the pipe will be a memory for another twenty years.

It is hard enough for me to understand this behavior on Jeru Creek. And that sense of violation persists. Each time we return to the cabin, we will look first to see if the pipe is back in the water. He may argue that no permanent damage is done to the creek by the wandering pcv, and that well may be true, at least to the physical structure of the stream, and in comparison to the impact of the wild water that courses through during the snowmelt floods.

The clarity of the actions, though, is much greater than my knowledge of my own behavior. Why, I ask myself, do I respond the way I do? The violation I see is painful to me. Inside, I want to go down to the creek, push the young people out, rip up the pipe, take it down the road, and lay it up the middle of his front yard. Why, then, am I either unwilling or unable to externalize my revulsion through my own version of eco-warriordom? Why do I walk away, complain to myself and to others, and then gradually adapt a softer image of what is out there, and perhaps hope for nature herself to respond appropriately come the spring floods? Is it simply because change happens and this is part of it? Is it because I acknowledge the legal right for the activity despite its distortion of the nature-centered view of the world? Is it because I want to avoid the confrontations that might result in an environment I come to in order to escape such conflict?

Once again I look to my childhood, and the model laid out before me. The first time my father took me fishing on Lawrence Lake we were to meet Paul Burton, another milkman for the Fort Lewis Dairy in Tacoma. I was about eleven or twelve. We had a special boat stored for us at the DeWitts' house on the lake. The DeWitts were an elderly couple that lived in a classic log home with a porch along the front and a steep decline of fifty or sixty feet down to the lake shore. The boat was unusual in its construction. Unlike almost every other craft on the lake, father's was not flat bottomed. The boat was shaped more like one of the New England dories, although not nearly so big I don't think (although I have never seen a real dory). The sides were an over-lapping set of long strips that gave it a unique look. Halfway down the rim of the boat on each side sat the holes for receiving thc oar locks, and in turn the oars. The exterior was a bright white.

Full of anticipation, we got up very early (at dawn in mid-April), drove the eight miles to the lake, passed the long lines waiting to get into the public areas, and went down the DeWitts' drive. We parked the car up by the house and carried the fishing rods, tackle boxes, net, and food down to the lake.

There was no boat there, at least not our boat. Someone had cut through the chain and taken the boat away.

I suppose that it is not hard to imagine the sense of violation we felt learning that the boat was gone. I was deeply disappointed, near tears. Paul Burton was enigmatic, showing no outward anger. My father was angry, although not bellicose or profane. Father went up to the DeWitt house and asked if Paul and I could use their boat for the day, so that we would not miss the fishing experience, while he went in search of his own missing craft. We hooked up father's small Johnson outboard motor to the DeWitts' rowboat, and Paul Burton and I began the day's fishing, trolling back and forth in front of the DeWitt home, no more than twenty or thirty feet off shore. We would do loops of about one hundred yards, from the dock down to an old snag protruding from the water, itself about the same distance from the beach. Occasionally we would tie up to the snag and still-fish for a while. All the time, though, we were searching for my father's return, we hoped with his boat in tow.

Paul and I caught a lot of trout that day, but our wait for the boat to return was in vain. Father did stop by several times on his canvassing of the other local lakes, scanning the surface with his binoculars for the very odd-shaped boat that was his alone.

The fact that my father did not bring the boat with him, though, does not mean he failed to find it. He did find it, on Clear

Lake—a somewhat larger body of trout fishing water about ten miles farther up in the Bald Hills. The boat was now a different color—yellow as I recall—hurriedly painted in an attempt to disguise it. But the boat was unmistakably his, the silhouette unique among the hundreds of others plying the lake. My father waited for the boat to come to shore, and then confronted the occupants with their misdeed, their violation of our property, but more important of our own day.

Perhaps even more hurtful than the loss of the boat and the loss of the day was learning who had broken the padlocked chain and hauled off our dory. The violators were two young men, sons of a family who lived no more than two miles from our home. I went to school with their sisters, and I faintly recall our own family visiting theirs once. They had—on a lark, perhaps—come across the boat and, recognizing its uniqueness, decided they wanted it for their own. They had painted it to disguise it, not realizing that its distinctive shape made it unhideable in the local area.

Once I learned about the source of the missing boat, I waited with some anticipation and delight, perhaps, for the punishment that would be laid on the boys. I was sure that my father would report them to the county sheriff and that they would be spirited off to jail, receiving their just due for their cavalier contempt for our property.

After we had come home and were sitting around the living room, I probed as to the action my father would take. He said that he was not going to take them to the police, nor was he going to report them. He had gone to their home and told their father. He was sure that the punishment there would be more harsh than they would receive at the hands of the law. The boat was returned, with much of the yellow paint removed, and some small financial retribution from the labor of the boys. I do remember the day of the return, the dory coming back in the bed of a pickup and the two young men struggling to take it into the basement through an outside entrance so that it could be repainted. I was not allowed to be outside to watch or to shame the boys, but I did observe from the living room window.

I cannot honestly say that my own responses to violation are tied to that day. In fact, I doubt that there are any direct connections between my father's reactions to the missing boat and my reactions to the disruptions in the Pack River Valley, although the model provided by my father during that day and across many others no doubt had a more subtle influence on who I am.

There is a bittersweet postscript to the violation produced by the theft of the boat. A year or two after that opening day disappointment, my father very suddenly died of a heart attack—he was only forty-three and I was only thirteen. During the remainder of the summer of his death the male friends of the family briefly rallied around to provide me with the kind of collective manly modeling they thought I now required. I was taken to the golf course in Tacoma many times, and given kind guidance as to how to hold both the club and my temper. I also was escorted fishing a couple of times.

During one of those fishing ventures I accompanied one of my father's contemporaries who was a descendant of one of the state's pioneer families. Fred had called and asked my recently widowed mother if I would be interested in a fishing trip. She of course replied in the affirmative. For us to go fishing, though, we needed a boat, and Fred had none. So, he asked my mother if he could borrow ours, the dory of my late father. My mother readily acceded so that I could have the experience to which I no longer would access with my father. We went fishing, although the details are fuzzy in my memory, and I returned home, probably with some trout for dinner and flush with the success of the fishing. I do remember a little awkwardness during the trip, probably to no little degree stemming from Fred's unfamiliarity with how to communicate with a teenage boy, and one just recently made fatherless at that. The gesture no doubt brought home also at least a subconscious sense of Fred's own mortality.

The stolen white dory that my father had relentlessly tracked down on one of the remote Bald Hills lakes never returned from the father-surrogate fishing trip with Fred. My fishing trip with Fred was the last time we saw the family fishing vessel. When we came home he asked if he could borrow it for another trip, and my mother said of course he could. I do not know where my father's friend took the boat, but I do know that he never brought it back. When I was a couple of years older and had my driver's license I would sometimes slowly creep by Fred's house in our car, looking for the boat, perhaps in the back on sawhorses, or hidden away in the dark of the garage. My mother, a young widow in a small town and needing to protect her place, her children, and her own aging, dependent mother, never felt that she could confront the man who took our boat. And, with a lingering, deep resentment, I thought about the boat and where it might be every time I went fishing by myself or took along my younger sister and we had to rent a rowboat from a lakeside marina.

The boat stolen from its moorage at the lake was returned, but with shame and chagrin and perhaps a lesson learned by the teenage thieves. The boat borrowed by a friend to take a fatherless boy fishing never came back. Which was the greater violation? I think the answer surely must be the one by the friend, for his grew out of the distortion of good will and failed resolve, and the advantage he gained by our family's weakness.

Which event provides the lesson I hope to give to the violations of time and tenor I now see in the Pack River Valley? The firm forgiveness of my father to the young men of Yelm who stole his boat seems much the better teacher.

15

Who Am I?

"BUT THIS IS NOT WHO I AM," she said weakly. The car door slowly swung open to reveal the depleted, aged shell of my mother. She had come home to die.

Three months earlier mother had called and asked me to help move her out of her house because she no longer could take care of herself. My wife and I drove across the state that weekend and found a place for her in a local care center. The center had admitted mother into their assisted living unit, where only minimal help was required. In the short time since then, though, her health had declined rapidly and she had so lost her will that her doctor had given her only a few weeks to live. Mother said she wanted to die in her home. She wanted to be there alone and independent, where she proudly had taken care of her family and herself for forty years, but that could not be.

Now, when my wife drove mother back home, a journey of only two miles from the care center, three women waited for her on the concrete front porch of her old one-story farmhouse. The unwanted welcomers were a nurse from Hospice, someone from the in-home care company we had hired, and a social worker. My mother was glad to enter the fir-shaded yard, and to see her own car still there. She still had the mental clarity to recognize the canyon between her current state and her memory of her life in that house.

She hesitated about leaving the car that brought her home because the reality of her rapid descent to death struck her full force in the presence of those unknown women on the steps of her home. Her terminal dependence on them removed from her the sense of who she was and what she represented. That person she knew so well, that powerful, independent woman who had been sheltered in her body, no longer existed except in the faint outlines of her will to control her own life, even as it ebbed away. Yet, it was that will to control her own life, and in that control to make a difference for other people, that both sustained her long beyond the doctors' predictions and provided the constant stream between those past days of her greatest vigor and those recent nights of her despair at dying.

It is true that in some very different ways, rivers and streams were important in my mother's life, although they did not have the same central focus as they seem to have had for me. She lived in Elm Creek, Nebraska, and she and my father farmed the banks of the Platte River, and she moved to the Nisqually River Valley. But her life was defined more by other, non-river events, those same events so overwhelming that they altered the course of the entire nation. Her life spanned nearly all of the twentieth century, born in 1911 and dying in 1996. Not only did she experience the changes these events brought, she was also able to embrace them in a way that allowed her to never leave small town Nebraska values and commitments, even while living in a different place. Her life was caught in a historic river, and she was swept along by the stream of events that altered her role as a woman and that defined her as a person.

I am not sure whether mother would be comfortable being called a "feminist" of any kind. Mother abjured being categorized or grouped, even though she joined groups; she always wanted to be known for herself, and never as one for whom others would feel sorry. She had intense pride in her independence and in her capacity to take care of herself. So when Ardith brought mother back to her own home she arrived at her front yard of forty years and hesitated. This woman who had lived by herself for four decades after her husband had died, who had done her own plumbing, made her own soap, and been a central figure of the core local community, now could not walk by herself, could not control her own bodily functions, could speak only erratically, could not drive, and knew she was coming home to die. It was not the dying she feared so much, but that she would die a different person than she had lived.

"It Was Not the Dying She Feared," Jo Hockenhull, 1999

In the later years of her life, mother was not easy to be with, especially in her frequent criticism that followed fast on our arrival at her home. The repeated stories and the emotional undercutting of the friends and family that she had loved and honored for her entire life were not the woman I remembered from her younger days. While she stayed involved in the community, she became increasingly inwardly focused. When an unforgiving side of her emerged in the context of a particular family crisis, it was painful to carry out the known obligations—the occasional visit, the Sunday evening phone call—because they were unpleasant, uncomfortable, and a signal of the need soon to enter into that most treacherous zone of taking away her independence.

My own reaction to mother's aging anger was to engage a kind of emotional neutrality, so that I could continue to talk with her, but also shield myself to some degree from the hurt, anguish, and frustration. It was a compromise, and not always one I felt good about.

In 1995, there accelerated this decline, both in her health and in the drift from the person she had been. A fall several years earlier had resulted in a hip replacement, but the fall seemed to come from a stroke. And after the fall, she was not the same, I think both because of the pain and because she seemed to have lost the will to carry on. She had had earlier illnesses, a heart attack, carotid artery problems, and a general weakness; in each case she had fought back and had done what was necessary to make herself as whole as possible. But this time, it was as if she had come to a realization that she had entered the final phase, and she was going to embrace it, not out of joy but out of inevitability. In 1995, this change was apparent to other people. I had several calls from neighbors and from her minister about events that were troublesome—confusion about the day, or a driving mishap or near mishap.

Then, in late June, mother herself called and said "John, you have to move me out of the house. I can't take care of myself anymore." We immediately arranged to go over that weekend. When we got there she was much less willing to consider the need for the change than she had been on the phone. She refused to move to the house of any of her children. She also refused to allow us to bring anyone into her home to take care of her. She agreed that we could find a place for her in McKenna, in her words, at the "old folks home," where her own mother had lived and died.

On short notice, we were able to find a room in McKenna which she could share until a single became available; she would be fed and there would be group activities and excursions. We thought that the opportunities for social interaction would open her up and perhaps restore some of her life energy. Perhaps the depression would ebb away. But, at the last minute, in a not un-expected development, she refused to go. With feelings of guilt, we cajoled and convinced her of its inevitability and reminded her of her own request.

The arrival of mother at the home deepened her depression considerably: her head slumped, her memory eroded, her unwill-ingness to communicate heightened. She was profoundly sad, and felt abandoned, even knowing the quandary in which she had placed us. Good friends visited her frequently, and our son Lamar lived in the area that summer and often stopped by to see how she was doing. But she refused to eat, she began to lose control of her bodily functions, and she had small strokes and increasing signs of congestive heart failure. Soon she was diagnosed to be at a level where more care was required, and then shortly thereafter moved to intensive nursing.

I was called by the staff at the care center and was told that the doctors felt that she had no more than two months to live, and perhaps less. Knowing my mother's independence and her pride and her love for her home, we decided to remove her from the nursing center and take her back to her Clark Road house. But in order to live at home, she required twenty-four-hour care, Hos-pice, and medical and nursing attention. Ardith went to Yelm to make those arrangements, and then brought mother back to her home where she searched for the resolve to be not just home, but to be herself in her home again.

Not long after mother came home, I took two weeks away from my job at the university to spend the time with her. Physically, she could barely stand, and needed assistance to rise from her chair. She could not control her bowels or bladder, and she had trouble eating. Emotionally, she was in a state of deepening sadness, refusing to respond or to interact with anybody around her, even to watch television. Mentally, the effects of the strokes were telling. She had difficulty talking, although she clearly could understand what others said to her. When she did talk she spoke in numbers and not in words. The numbers seemed to be symbolic representations of words, most often names. I was number one hundred.

During those two weeks I wove my time with mother in and among the duties of the caregivers. I often sat on the couch with my laptop in front of me, working on a paper or writing memoranda, always present in her sight when she woke. I talked with her about our family, and about memories I had of stories she had told me, and events I remembered from childhood. A leak sprung in the ceiling of one of the bedrooms and I spent the better part of the day in the attic and on the roof patching it against the next storm. I put plastic on the windows of the pump house and walked the fence lines to make sure that no wayward steer could enter the yard. I ordered a new refrigerator since hers no longer functioned.

After each maintenance foray I made a full report to my mother and she would nod in approval, albeit always grumbling about the cost. Eventually, she improved to where we would watch sports on television, and I would comment on the progress of the game. But often I would just sit there, holding her hand, and trying to lift her health and her spirits with my will. The attention and the stimulation at home, and the repeated reminders of love, had a visible effect on mother's own will. She began working harder to recover from the strokes, even though the decline of her heart apparently continued unabated. Every once in a while, though, the despair would overcome her, and through her tears she would say to me that she "didn't want to die this way."

The days of constant care for my mother lifted us both. Both the cynicism and anger of her later years and my retreat into an emotional neutrality to manage the pain disappeared in those two weeks. Perhaps the strokes had wiped clear her anger-filled memory, or the pre-death peace so many report had descended, but she was so benign and tranquil that I at first had trouble recognizing and trusting it. The love was overwhelming, and it flooded away the fear and reluctance with which I had entered into those two weeks. It completely restored the emotional basis of our relationship. That restoration made her death harder for me in the short run, but prevented what might have been a lifelong guilt about her leaving with our love unsettled.

In the weeks after my stay, mother made what the caregivers called a "miraculous recovery." We returned to Yelm and took her to church, and she walked down the aisle by herself to the applause of the congregation. The medical people removed her from Hospice, no longer diagnosing her as terminal. The resurgent emotional health, though, masked the continuing physical decline. As I became hopeful at the prospects of her continued life, I also despaired as to how I was going to manage her long-term health care with expenses now surging near $10,000 a month. I knew that as soon as we could no longer afford to keep her in her home, she would die some other place.

Then, in the middle of January, her final slide into death began. Two or three times a week the paramedic team from down the road would be called and she would be taken to Olympia to the hospital. In late January we visited her in Yelm and stayed at our friends, the Schornos. In the middle of the night the phone rang with the word that she was once again being taken to the hospital in Olympia. We got into our car and drove through the rain darkened Nisqually reservation to the hospital. We met her there in the emergency room. By this time she was again fully alert, pumped full of oxygen and pain reducers. She was giving orders to the doctors, especially about taking no extraordinary efforts to revive her. She was perky and positive, although no less fatalistic about her future.

We waited until her release about three in the morning, and with her in the car started the drive back to Yelm and to her home. As we gained ground toward her house my mother started talking to me. "John," she again told me, "I didn't want to die like this." "Mother," I replied softly with some sadness-tinged bemusement, "How do you want to die?" Her answer was clear. "I want to die at home, in my sleep, in my own bed, and have them haul me out feet first."

A couple of hours later, after having settled mother in her bed, we drove back across the state to Pullman. In a few days the phone rang in the late evening with the news that she had died. We left early the next morning and returned to Yelm to make the final arrangements. She is buried in Puyallup, next to my father, in the plot reserved for her forty years earlier.

Only a few days transpired before we held the memorial service in the local church. Mother had always said she did not want a service because she thought no one would show up, and she did not want the family to be embarrassed. I disobeyed my mother. Even on very short notice, the church was full, as we all had anticipated. Adults who many years ago had been in her first grade class—an Episcopal priest, the county sheriff, other local teachers, farmers, and people she had supported financially through school—and others whose life she had touched, filled the pews to overflowing and spilled into the choir loft and out the back of the sanctuary.

In the eulogy at the service I told some stories about her life, and I ended with the description of the trip back from the hospital, through the wet early morning, and her will as to how she would die. I said she had died the way she wanted to die, on her terms, and where she wanted to be. Her seeming control of her own death was testament to the power she expressed in her management of her life. And her death was a refutation of her own fear about that loss of control. She lived and died the same way, a clear reflection of what she saw herself to be.

My mother's need to represent clearly her own conception of who she "really" was—and her capacity to focus on that fundamental center and to control the very end of her life—has given me frequent cause to reflect on my own life, and in the context of the themes of many of these essays, on both the real and the metaphoric role of rivers in defining who I am and, even more importantly, in my understanding of that person.

The river is both shaper and revealer of the self. The river has profoundly influenced who I am, what I believe, and what I want to be, but even more importantly, what I know about myself. In trying to decipher the river's influence I come to realize the obvious, that like the river, every stone I overturn reveals a person— sometimes me, sometimes someone else, and sometimes a me that I either fail to recognize or wish not to acknowledge.

The self's washing from the river is mediated by people, like my mother, and not just in the physical sense of the dam, or the culvert, or the bridge, or the riprap along the side. The river has meaning in my life because of how it structures and is structured by my relationships with family, with friends, and with people who do not know me but are affected by my actions. As much as I might want to, I cannot remove the river from my sense of who I am in reference to other people, my constructions of them, and theirs of me. Even when I wander alone up Jeru Creek and pause at Traveler's Rest for a moment of introspection or meditation, what I often think about is the quality of my connections to other people rather than the river. I struggle to define clearly in my own mind who I am and what I believe and how I act and how to account for the gaps between them. Being on the river gives me the freedom to wander in my mind, and it often confronts me with those unexpected choices that define who I really am. The river clarifies those definitions of my self partly because there is an absence of complexity in those moments.

Al Kitchel, a wonderful friend, a dentist in a Seattle suburb, a roommate from the first year of college, loves to tell a story from our early years. One summer during college we both were in Tacoma, working to pay for the next year's tuition. After work on Friday we left Tacoma and drove to his home in Forks, on the ocean side of the Olympic Peninsula. We arrived late, and then got up very early to take a fishing trip into the Olympic Mountains, along the Bogachiel River. We had wonderful fishing, lots of trout and beautiful weather. We had a great time but, as ex-high school athletes and marginal college basketball players, we could not escape our competitive juices. Eight or ten miles up the river we came to a beautiful pool, its entrance marked by the rapid and steeply descending riffle that brought the food to the trout deep in the green waters. The back side of the pool rose steeply in a small cliff that topped out with the old growth cedar towering above. We stood on a gravel bank, with the sun at our backs. Lurking in the pool, submerged barely below the surface but extending to the river bottom, was a giant log.

At that time in my fishing life, I had no idea about fly fishing. We used spinners and nightcrawlers, or sometimes just the nightcrawlers alone, and drifted them down the riffle into the pool, watching for cutthroat and rainbow. Al repeatedly enjoys telling of my frustration at a recurring inability to hook the fish, losing my worm and several times my spinner on the log. Al claims, although I have only a faint memory of it myself and am not sure if that memory comes from Al's retelling or from the incident itself, that my frustration reached a peak. I became so angry that I grabbed the red felt hat from my head, threw it on the ground, stomped on it several times, picked it up, and then took a big bite out of the brim.

That's who I was at that time…needing affirmation, evidence of my success, and proof of my abilities even or perhaps especially in the presence of my closest friends. But I acknowledge that it also remains some of who I now am, and who my family recognizes when the lawnmower fails for the fourth time in an afternoon, or the last sheet of plywood for a cabin wall is cut too small because I hurried so I could get back to the paperwork waiting on the desk at the office.

While funny to Al Kitchel, trying to eat my hat is neither a memory nor a recognition that flatters me. And, my continuing embarrassment itself is a sign that the same strain works within me still. It was later in my life when I recognized that with family or friends the catching is not the reason for the fishing, nor is the catching the foundation of the friendship. The friendship is the foundation for a special kind of fishing, and the catch lasts a lifetime. But who I am now was clear to Al Kitchel years ago, and so as he uses it to explain to others who I am, and the best I can hope for is that my frustration at failure revealed then and now is both an incentive to do better in ways that are not just for me, but a benefit for others, and a way for me to be reminded of who I really am, if not who I want to be.

I grew up not just being frustrated at failure, whether on the river or in the classroom, but also with an accompanying sense that even more important than doing something right was doing the right something. Sometime in high school, before I was old enough to drive myself, I was invited to go fishing on the

Nisqually River with a friend and his family. I rode my bike from our house to theirs, a distance of about two miles, down Clark Road, through town, and then out the north side on Canal Road, so named because it paralleled a multi-mile ditch that diverted water from the river upstream and carried it down to where it dove into the river again through the Centralia Power House turbines. I spent Saturday night with the Johnsons, sleeping upstairs in a two story frame house overlooking Yelm Creek.

We got up early on Sunday and took the truck out to the river, to a place near what locally was called Devil's Slide, because of the gravelly steep cliff beside the river. We did a kind of fishing which I never had done before—we were after the searun cutthroat, the anadromous cousin of the steelhead trout, also called harvest trout by some, because the runs often are in late summer or early fall. The Johnsons taught me how to fish for the searun cutthroat. First, we went down to Yelm Creek behind their house and caught crawdads and took the crustaceans' tails, then extracted the white meat from the tails and threaded it on the size eight or ten hook. We drifted the shucked crawdad tail deep into the bottom of the river pools where it floated slowly a foot or so above the gravel until it was taken by the trout.

I remember the experience well because it was my first time on the Nisqually River, and my first time fishing for big trout. I had an old fiberglass rod, maybe five-and-a-half feet long, with the bottle green opaque look typical of that style. The worn four-pound monofilament line was coiled on a cheap Zebco reel, the kind with the closed face and the bullet nose and the line emerging from the pin hole at the top. What I remember is that my line was broken early in the trip and that I tied it together with a square knot, with the frayed ends of the knot protruding obviously and impeding the smooth flow of the line through the ferrules.

The early morning was bright and beautiful, and I approached a pool with rod and crawdad in hand. To my great surprise and joy I hooked and landed an eighteen-inch searun cutthroat. But as I reveled in that success, I had a slow dawning of a guilt-tinged awareness that I was not even supposed to be on the river that Sunday morning. That was the Sunday morning I had promised to be in church, to be an usher and to take the collection.

Our church was small, a traditionally shaped Methodist building on the main street of Yelm, with the narrow and pointed steeple in front, and the long rope for pulling the bell hanging down in the church entry. Traditional Methodist churches (the people, not the buildings) in the late 1950s were pretty heavy on guilt, and when coupled with the omnipresent morality play of two grandmothers whose idea of sin included the slightest transgression of omission or forgetfulness, the guilt spread through my fishing joy, dampening it and suppressing the special flavor of the day.

Church did not start until eleven, and it was only 8:30 when the cutthroat gave himself up. But I gave up too. I asked Mr. Johnson to take me back to their house, and I rode my bike home with my trophy dangling from a stick on the handlebars and my fiberglass stick strapped to the back. I made it to the church on time. And I ushered and I collected, and I felt a little sanctimonious in a teenage sort of way, but also a little shortchanged, not only because I had given up my first successful venture on the big river, but also because no one there knew of my sacrifice.

That guilt-driven bicycle ride home also is part of who I am. The teenage years are said to be the formative ones, when we acquire our fundamental values that sustain us through the rest of life. The choice between church and cutthroat was neither earthshaking nor heaven shaking, I am sure. Had I not showed up, someone else would have taken collection and ushered, and I would not have been the worse for it in a fundamental moral sense, or probably not in the eyes of the other Methodists either, or even in the view of my grandmothers had they been allowed to find out.

I had not yet realized, or perhaps had not yet rationalized, the temple of the trout, the cutthroat church in which there resides the awesome sense of the spiritual and of the non-ordained, non-ritualized religious litany of the river. The river and the wind and the birds merge their voices in a hymn Charles Wesley could not hope to sing or compose. The arched, green-boughed cover over the rock-strewn pews provides resting and kneeling sites for the angling congregation. But even to this day, I suppose, were I to be on the river with my fly rod, perhaps now more aesthetically pursuing the trout, and were I to remember an obligation I had made, even a trivial one, the grandmother, Methodist-honed sense of guilt would rise up and send me on my way—perhaps no longer by bike—to wherever I am supposed to be, hoping to get to that church on time.

The religious metaphor of course does extend further. Just as one can be alone in the community of a church, in that kind of personal experience and relationship I have read about, the real sense of who I am on the stream comes when I wade into the river alone. Standing in the middle of the pool, or down near the bottom of a run, or fording a treacherous high water with nothing else around save the rushing stream and the graveled shore, isolates me both physically and emotionally. The horizontal structure of the river pushes me up and out of the layered water, standing there as if caught, temporarily frozen, in suspension of lift-off. Who I am in juxtaposition to the river is rarely more clear—the interloper, the orthogonal intruder, the unstable and insecure trespasser on the algae-covered stones of the river bottom. That simplicity, that forced clarity, helps me understand who I am.

As my experience with my dying mother taught me, there is, of course, nothing more simple, more clarifying than the prospect of impending death. The Nisqually River witnessed my surest encounter with death, at least in my own mind. As a young child, I had shown an allergic reaction to yellow jackets. A single sting would cause my hand to swell to where I couldn't use it, or if on my face, would close an eye. When stung I would be watched closely, sometimes taken to the doctor in town or to the hospital in Olympia or Tacoma, for some antidote to the poison. We lived on five acres of a former small truck garden. It was gravelly soil, and the moles made it their home as well. Those mole holes provided an underground den for the yellow jackets. My job was to mow the lawn, which in the summer I often did barefoot, a magnet for the yellow jacket on a feeding foray. Each time I was stung the reaction seemed to get worse, and I had been warned that soon I might need the desensitization treatment of multiple inoculations over an extended period. The cure loomed more ominous than the disease.

My father died in the summer after my eighth grade. Not too long after his death the youth group of the local Methodist church scheduled a hike along the Nisqually River, I think partly as a way of assuaging my sorrow over the loss of a parent. We went down to the river, accompanied (and driven) by the Reverend Leps, pastor of the church.

A couple of carloads of us went to the river near where Yelm Creek empties in, and began to hike up a trail along the river to a place where we might picnic and, I suppose, engage in some teenage meditation. The Nisqually River is glacier fed, and when it is hot up on Mt. Rainier, the river sometimes rises. The river also has a dam or two on it, and the dams divert water to produce electricity. So when the water is crashing through the turbines and back into the river, or when Mt. Rainier is melting, or when the dam spillways are opened, the Nisqually changes from a shallow stream to a fearsome roil. The trail sat on a long ledge that runs aside the river, some six to eight feet about the low water flow, elevated enough to stay out of reach of the high water. The shore side of the trail was a very steep hillside, with tree branches and bushes hanging out, causing the walker to duck and dodge.

I was moving along the trail with Elsie Sherman, a friend from school and the church, one of those quasi-sisters that you start out with in the first grade and end up graduating from college with, but now see only once every five years at a wedding or a funeral that calls people home, but with whom there is a fundamental kind of tethering of your past and your present. We were laughing and talking, and I noticed that some of the people in front of us were making a commotion but I did not pay much attention. Jim Raab was right in front of me, and I saw him swat at something, but I kept going. By that time, though, the line of hikers had halted, and those ahead of us tried to ward off the wasps that had begun to attack them. Stacked up behind us was another small group of hikers, effectively thwarting any kind of retreat. The sudden stasis left Elsie and me standing directly over the yellow jackets' home. We were attacked fiercely, but we had no place to go, not even into the river, for it was at flood stage.

We finally fought our way through the line behind us and ran back toward the cars. We didn't know where to go or what to do. I believed that I was going to die soon, overwhelmed by poison flooding through my body. If one bee sting would send me to the hospital, what would all of these do to me but kill me? The minister knew I was allergic and got me in his car. We headed back to town where there was a clinic. The trip to town was about a fifteen-minute drive, and all of the time I thought that I soon would die. The minister drove at a dangerous speed, I remember, reaching ninety miles an hour once we made it to the blacktop road. But the clinic in Yelm was closed and the doctor was out of town. So we headed to Olympia, about fifteen miles away, at a rate surpassing that which had seen us enter Yelm. By this time, though, I remember a kind of calm had started to descend over me. I do not know if that was the result of what I remember to be a constant mumbled prayer from the minister, or from the inevitability of death I saw, if not from the yellow jackets then from the breakneck voyage to the hospital.

We got to the hospital and I was still breathing. Most of the stings had been on my head, but I could see and talk and hear. We went into the emergency room and the doctor looked at me and told me to sit over on the side of the room. I presumed that he had concluded that there was little they could do for me at such an advanced stage of termination. But a half-hour later I was invited into a private room and was examined. They counted the stings on my head—as I remember, there were over one hundred of them, although perhaps it was only fifty, but none of them swollen to more than a pimple. They gave me some pills to take home with me in case there was some kind of delayed reaction, but I never used them.

Why did I live? I am not sure. I have no fundamental belief in the miracle of divine intervention for a thirteen-year old unfortunate enough to walk into a hive. But who knows? Some have suggested that over the years the stings in our front yard naturally immunized me, but that was a rather sudden and extreme desensitization. And later that summer I was tested for the possibility of kidney problems, related perhaps to the organ's work in screening the poison from my system. Ever since then, though, whenever I am stung I feel some pain, and I pull out the stinger if I can see it. But the swelling rarely passes that produced by the bite of a mosquito.

But each new sting reminds me of the Nisqually River and of that time when I thought I was surely going to die, close in the wake of my father's death, and of when I was retrieved by luck, or by the beauty of the natural processes of the body, or by a gift I do not feign to ken. But never do I forget that each day, each walk along a river, has been more than I once thought I would have.

Do these river stories bring me closer to a sense of who I am in the same certainty that my mother carried? Only in retrospect is that window open. Each new trek to a stream provides a surprise of self-assessment and self-revelation. When I think I know myself, another face appears in the mirror, and not always is it the face I want or expect to see. Yet, my mother's death and her commitment to the preservation of her self do intertwine with my river walking. In the starkness of the river surface there is both time and clarity to reflect on the answer to the question of who I am. But I now know that the searching for an answer, even in the river's depths, surely cannot produce the same sense of certainty of self as did my mother's call to her own death.

16

Rivers of Change

"WELL, I GUESS WE'RE OUT OF HERE," Ardith responded. I had just told my wife of thirty-two years about the call from Colorado Springs. Several hours earlier Ardith had been offered a position in the public schools in the beautiful Front Range city that soon was to be our new home. She had received her message from the Colorado Springs School District telling her that they wanted her to become a principal in one of their elementary schools. But the caller also told her that since the superintendent wanted to announce the appointment that night at a school board meeting, she had to give them an answer in two or three hours.

I had been to Colorado Springs for several interviews on the University of Colorado campus there, and I had spent a day in Seattle with the Chancellor for more talks. Although I had not yet received an offer for the position of Vice Chancellor, Ardith and I thought one soon might be forthcoming. We also knew that the Chancellor and the chair of the search committee still wanted to spend a day at Washington State University where I then was Dean of the College of Liberal Arts—apparently to see if any skeletons would come out of the campus closet.

After I heard from Ardith that she had received her offer, I immediately phoned the Chancellor in Colorado, and told her our situation. If I could not receive substantial encouragement nearly immediately, and given the very short time frame available, Ardith would need to decline the school district position and I would have no choice but to withdraw from consideration for the job on the campus. The Chancellor said she would call me back in a few minutes. When she did call she hesitated a few seconds and then said, "Well, consider our conversation in Seattle an informal offer." I thanked the Chancellor and then phoned Ardith who called the superintendent and accepted the job, and "we were out of here," in mind, if not yet in body. I knew that it all could unravel, since the Chancellor's visit to our campus had not yet happened, and no offer in Colorado is official until approved by the Regents. But, we went ahead anyway, preparing ourselves for the coming upheaval in our lives.

I still wonder how all of that happened. At least on the surface, change is not something with which I have been particularly conversant. We had lived in the same town for twenty-four years, moving just once, and then a distance of only four miles. I was Dean of the college for nearly a dozen years when the average tenure across the country is said to be somewhere between three and five. Ardith was principal of the same elementary school for as long as I was Dean. We had been in the same church for two decades. We have been married for over thirty years. We have had our cabin for over twenty years. I know that our friends and colleagues expected that we would live in the same house and work in the same jobs until we retired, itself at least another decade away. Deep down, I guess I probably felt much the same way. But, the world around us changes, and for some reason so did we.

With lots of regrets and no little sadness, we left that home, and that town, and those jobs, and all of those colleagues and friends and memories of the good times and bad we had had with them. We moved to new challenges, a new city more than a thousand miles distant, and a new home. Still I sometimes wonder why and how we felt that move was the right thing to do. When things become difficult, or I get tired or depressed or lonely, I once more search through the decision, asking myself if the change was what we should have done. I always reach the same conclusion, though—the uprooting dislocation and the growth-producing, energy-demanding, risk-taking challenge that comes with it were exactly the right thing for me to do.

What gave me the sense that after so long in the same place I could make this change and survive, and perhaps even grow? I do not think that at the time I was fully self-conscious about what gave me that impulse, but now I look back and I see a little more clearly the wellsprings of that sharp turn in our life.

Ardith, this culture-altering woman, child-loving, compassionate beauty, left her friends and her family to give me the strength I needed to make my own change. Ardith had always said that she embraced change, and wanted to try some new adventures, but I do not think either of us knew how difficult it would be for her. Only in the retrospect produced by the first year's passing is it clear how much she gave up to make it possible for me to leave Pullman and for her to take on the challenge of a new school, itself in the midst of its own evolution.

Around the time of our leaving, the local daily paper in Pullman twice acknowledged Ardith's central role in the community. Shortly before we left, a front-page carried a story with pictures that showed a nearly finished elementary school, the headline over which read: "The School that Ardith Built." With several others, Ardith had shepherded the concept and construction of that school through the labyrinth of local parental, community, and taxpayer obstacles. She traveled the Northwest to find the marbleized world map on the entry floor, and the concrete sculptured animals embedded around the building. And she cajoled me into our gift of several dozen ceramic fish formed by a local artist. The school's brightly colored trout hang prominently on the foyer wall of the building, testament to the joining of her love of the children there, and my love for the moving water where those sleek creatures are found in nature.

To the few of us who worked and lived with Ardith during her years as principal at "old Franklin," the new building will always stand as symbol to her capacity to deal compassionately with conflict in the pursuit of vision. But the more telling story was the editorial in the *Daily News* that appeared not long after we had left Pullman. Its headline read "Forever Changing How We Envision Principals." The text referred to her care and

Ardith next to her Mother's Day present

understanding, her tolerance and her embracing of diversity, and her love of the children and her building full of a faculty unmatched in its commitment to a culture of both affection and excellence. To be sure, the school's children had great scores on achievement tests, and an innovative curriculum and wonderfully dedicated teachers, and Ardith herself had received awards of achievement both in the profession and in the community. But many parents told me the palpable trait of the school was the overwhelming feeling they experienced on entering the building. They knew that they had found a place that was child-centered, that held no preconceptions of who would achieve. In some years as many as twenty-five different languages were native to the students there, but they all felt at home when going through the front door.

Neither of us expected the public recognition she received that last year. I do know that her visible actions were simply the veneer over a much stronger commitment and a much deeper sea of hidden deeds into which she would drag me, often reluctantly. Few know the weekends when she brought into our home the children of single-parent families so that a mother could make a needed trip, or the slumber parties she hosted because the child's home was too small, or the Christmas mornings she woke me before dawn so we could drive across town to leave a ribbon be-decked bicycle outside the door of an international family that could not afford to buy it themselves. Often her acts of good were presented to me as fait accompli. She knew I would grumble and object to the intrusion into the peace to which I retreated on holi-days, weekends, or evenings. But she also knew that I believed she was doing the right thing, and that I was proud of her, and I knew that she had more courage and commitment than I.

I don't mean to idolize Ardith or our relationship. She is strong-willed and a powerful personality and we sustain our commitment to each other through conscious, intentional deci-sions about some of those shared spaces into which we will not enter. Writing about her is difficult for me, for I shy from the re-alism that might abrade the smooth contours of her core. I could come to even this superficial level of description only in this last chapter and only after we had been through this change and the clarity and renewal it produced. I thought recently about a con-versation I had a few years ago. After relating some of the stories in other chapters of this book, and describing my relationship with Ardith, a young friend, who had recently divorced her hus-band and was self-consciously assessing her own life, said to me in a tone of some resentment and anger: "You are so lucky, you have a perfect life." I said to her, "No, I don't. But I do have a good life, and even that takes a lot of hard work." Fortunately, Ardith knows my imperfections and she usually tolerates them. Part of that very hard work for her was accommodating my need to leave Pullman. We agreed that we would not go unless we found jobs that were good for both of us. And implicit, too, was a sense of a need for another environment in which streams and rivers are spawned, and where the horizon provides a constant reminder of their birth. We found all of that in Colorado Springs, and we found some new times and new demands for the hard work to make our life good. We also know that we lost a lot, too. Moving to a large, new city separated us physically from what we knew, those whom we loved, and the places that provided our daily referents.

Especially those who knew us well, and who had some sense of the restlessness we felt, were stunned at our choice of Colorado Springs. Although pretty conservative in our life-style, by most accounts we probably can be characterized as social, political, and religious liberals. But Colorado Springs has developed a national reputation for a conservative, fundamental, Christian-based public life. State expenditure limitations, anti-gay rights initiatives, a libertarian owned and editorially controlled daily newspaper, and a long legacy of failed school bond and levy proposals had created an aura of opposition to the kinds of values that we have affirmed for decades. I must admit that our calls to friends who had worked and lived in Colorado Springs and our reading of the reports raised some nagging doubts about leaving the comfort of our friends, home, and social support in Pullman. Could we possibly find a way to make this new place fit us and our needs and beliefs in the way to which we had grown accustomed?

While on a dusk-encroaching walk on one of our visits to Colorado Springs before taking the job there, Ardith and I saw an old stone church downtown, not far from the hotel where we were staying. The building was visible from around the city with its shiny metallic roofing on the cupola-like top, and the more than hundred year old sanctuary seemed anchored firmly in place by the heavy, rough, stone arches at the front. Like our home church in Pullman, it was a Congregational church. The next day happened to be Sunday, and we decided to attend the service to see if this might be the place that would fill our need to build a value-based home outside of our jobs.

We sat through the service, and we felt a sense of community there, even though we later learned that the congregation had just gone through a divisive controversy over the role of gays in the church and the propriety of gay marriage. At the end of the service, after the benediction, the bulletin indicated that everyone should sing together the music printed on the inside of the back cover of the hymnal. We turned to the song, and listened with some amazement and no little emotion as the congregation sang the same verses from Micah that for years I had carried on a small slip of paper in my wallet.

I am not consciously a believer in "signs" or messages directing my life (although I will admit to reading my horoscope many mornings). But that moment in that church was pivotal in our capacity to make this change. The church seemed like it might be another place we could call home, a physical referent with a mix of people and values that could create the sense of identification that might bind us to that place. Now, a year later, along with our home and our two work places, that church place continues to be a focal point of continuity across the two very different locations. We are not yet deeply integrated into the church, and the congregation has experienced another divisive conflict ironically growing out of a formal peacemaking process. But we are growing some friendships and some comfort and the formal and informal affirmations of the church there confirm our original impressions about what we would find.

How did this evening walk help us make the change in our life? We left a place and went to another place. And, it was the sense of place that provided the wrap around the life we led. And, the life we led was defined by the experiences and the people who had helped construct us through the years. And one part of that place in Pullman was the church in which we had participated for nearly two decades. In the 1970s we were attracted to that Congregational church by its social and political positions consistent with our own understanding of Christian tenets, by its spiritual base, and by the strong sense of community in a relatively small group of parishioners. After we had joined the Pullman church, we were told that we now were members of the town's "liberal" congregation. The label was not important to us, for we had found a deep sense of caring about other people, both inside and outside of the church, and about our children and the kind of people into which they would grow. Hillary Clinton's now near cliché of the "village" raising our children could find no more appropriate model than the small UCC Church in Pullman.

Our sons went on CROP walks with us to raise money for worldwide hunger needs, they worked in orphanages in Mexico, and they were taught to care for other people. I think nothing better reflects the core values that we affirmed, the church in Pullman proclaimed, and the congregation in Colorado Springs sang, than that verse from Micah:

> He has showed you what is good; and what does the Lord require
> of you, but to do justice, to love kindness and to walk humbly with
> your God? (Micah 6:8)

It was comfortable there, in that church, knowing that there was a place and a community that was a home for our values, where those beliefs were rarely challenged. The church was a place to which we could and would retreat from those personal and professional dangers that cause the discomfort that produces both growth and threat.

So moving to Colorado Springs, to a different place, was much more than a simple professional relocation, more than a new challenge to energize the remainder of our work lives. But we

also know that this change in our personal life, as real and immediate as it is to us, pales in contrast to that constantly shifting
world around us, whether in our jobs, in our town, or in some
place else more remote. And, I think that it is because of the instability and unpredictability of that world that I would often go to
our Jeru Creek cabin in the apparently idyllic wilderness. There I
would search for an escape from that dislocation, from that
change, and from the tumultuous elements of our daily life that
require the constant adaptation to the unexpected. The world we
all live in is both a source of disruption for us as individuals and a
barometer of what we have lived through. I was born during
World War II, a "war baby" whose life has been played out in what
has seemed like an exponentially expanding social universe. Everything I knew to be true and constant, everything that provided
the stable foundation for my values and my actions, will exhibit a
different form tomorrow than it does today. And each of those
perturbations in my life seems to interact with every other to
project a personal trajectory that only the most prescient can
claim to clarify.

In many ways, I go to Lagniappe, to Jeru Creek, and to the
Pack River to escape those changes, to search for stability in some
deeply grounded roots through which the same nutrients that
formed me years ago can again provide me with the energy for a
robust future. Cable television, cellular phones, and microwave
ovens are either unable to follow me up river, or I intentionally
leave them at the gate of my emotional transition on the way in to
the Pack River Valley. And the memory and the knowledge of that
privileged place provide another reason I have been able to move
on to a different place.

Ardith and I both grew up in early post-depression families,
in personal and community economies that were marginal, but
nonetheless seemed secure. Neither of us wanted for food or
clothing, although what we had was basic and unadorned. Given

the instability and the insecurity our parents had experienced in their youth, both families driven from the Midwest dustbowl, we each had a remarkably stable childhood. To be sure, we knew economic and family disruptions in our respective homes. My father died early, and Ardith's family lived through some significant financial challenges. Even through these domestic earthquakes, though, there seemed a constant of values and expectations for us provided by extended family and the larger villages in which we lived.

I think our own memories of the security and stability of home is one reason we came to the Pack River Valley. We wanted to have a place that combined the constancy of our own youths and the simplicity of the times in which we spent them. Out of that combination we had the hope that we would find emotional comfort and that our sons would find in the natural and the familial referents around Jeru Creek the source of the values and the commitments that would guide their lives.

It is naive, of course, to think that any wilderness retreat can provide complete escape from either the changes of the modern world, or the vagaries of its impact on one's internal globe. If change fails to lie in wait for you, it chases you down instead. There have been lots of changes along Jeru Creek, and there have been many changes in us as we come to it each time for personal restoration.

Perhaps the greatest recoloring of my worldly lens has come in how I respond to what we have seen happen around us. For this new view, I must give much credit to my older son Forrest. I will admit that I have reacted with internal horror and external outrage at a lot of the things that have happened near our cabin, and that as a result have changed this little haven to which I escape. These portents of the future have disturbed my sense of stability and my hope for continuity in what has seemed to be a concrete referent for my life. But Forrest has taught me that change is part of the order of things, that "change happens."

When we first moved to Jeru Creek, we had the only cabin there, save for a sheltered trailer across the Pack River road one half mile down near the mouth of the creek where it goes into the river, and an unsided log frame structure that the Craigs used for a month late each summer. So, every unfamiliar person was an intruder; in my mind, no one else belonged there, and it was our creek and our river. While other people owned the land around us, I tried to protect all of it as if it were my own, questioning anyone who camped on it, or seemed to threaten it while hunting for huckleberries and firewood.

With increasing speed, the Jeru Creek Valley and its environs have been on a roller coaster of change produced by other people, some like us, and some with very different goals. Apart from a log house up the road a ways, when built I am not sure, I think the first people to follow us to the creek were the Dengerinks. Hal, Joan, Erin, and Kris were neighbors in Pullman, and very good friends. Several times they came with us to the creek for a weekend, and later they came by themselves to use our cabin. One day Hal asked me if I had any objection if they talked with Jim Brown about buying the cabin site next to ours. We offered no resistance, in fact thinking it to our advantage to have other people we knew and trust around either when we were there or not there.

The Dengerinks' cabin went up in due time, and so did the Lovrichs', other friends from Pullman. Even more recently, several more cabins have appeared across the creek, and the Craigs' shelter is now supplemented by a two-story home built by someone from Sandpoint. Down near The Meadow, a place where our children had run relay races, picked wild strawberries, crept up on deer and moose, and where I had sat in the sun, absorbing the soul-healing heat of its rays reflected off the mica- and granite-particled sand, there now is a horse corral, at one point planned to be a ranch. We have been fortunate, though, for those who have come to the Jeru Creek canyon generally have been good people who share a love for the area and a willingness to act as stewards within the altered state we have created.

But it is different nonetheless. We now have a community, rather than the isolation to which we thought we had retreated. No longer is the noise on the other side of the creek the exhaust of a lost berry picker's truck. The peace-disturbing sounds are from people like us, who want isolation and oddly look for it in a place where many others are also settling for their retreat.

The irony for me is that in a time when scholars and pundits decry the loss of community and the decline of the civic culture, as a political scientist I study the capacity for people to participate effectively in that community. Yet, I run away from it for silence and solace at Jeru Creek. But the changes taking place at Jeru Creek prove to me that there can be no escape from community and the obligations to others.

In the last few years our cabins have been increasingly subject to vandalism and theft. We have had break-ins that leave the cabin interior exposed to the harsh winter elements. Broken windows, stolen generators and chain saws, and the emotional anguish of intrusion jaundice our views of this one-time private world. But, nonetheless, because of another change, we felt more secure, at least for a time. The cowboy ferrier who started the ranch in The Meadow was a good person who in his solitude also had a community view of Jeru Creek and the canyon and those who live there. He and his wife protected our space, turning away potential invaders who otherwise would enter with impunity. But now they have sold their place because there are too many people there, and from our newly distant Colorado home we faced with some uncertainty the prospect of other neighbors at Jeru Creek who may not be so benign. So, we and the Hills and the Lovrichs have pooled our resources to purchase the little ranch and its small cabin and corrals.

It wasn't the same at the cabin, with horses and fences on the hillside above us, and a corral in The Meadow that once first signaled our arrival at isolation. But what we do have that remains from when we first came to Jeru Creek—the cabin, the stream, the family history of our children maturing with values I admire—will likely stay longer because living with change is much better than ignoring it.

Arnold Schwartzenegger is rumored to be building a castle somewhere around Lake Pend Oreille, the final home of the Jeru Creek water that cascades in front of the cabin. A landowner ran a white plastic pipe down the middle of Jeru Creek, an angry scar in front of all of the cabins, to demonstrate his water rights on the stream. We and the Hills bought some more land across the creek to try to protect ourselves. Every time our two sons leave the cabin for the last time at the end of summer, we fear that it may be for a very long absence. Forrest is fighting a genetic disease of the auto-immune system. Lamar is out of college now, married, and in graduate school. And we have taken an opportunity to re-direct the course of our lives. We don't know that this is the right decision, but we will live with it, for we have no choice. Saying "yes" means there is no chance to go back to "no."

Change does happen, and when it does, it is rarely in the way we expect. Sometimes we walk up to change and turn away, with reluctance or with relief, or even in ignorance at the possibility that rests there. Sometimes change overwhelms us, washing across in such force and magnitude that we are carried along not knowing it has happened. Sometimes we grab hold of change and hold on, and other times we try to decide ourselves where we are going. As the change happens outside, we change inside too. And that internal change alters the eye with which we view the onrushing currents of the future.

In revising these last few words, I am on an airplane, flying from Denver to Spokane. I am returning to Jeru Creek for the first

Jaci and Amanda, learning to fish

time in nearly a year. Forrest and Lamar will be there, at Lagniappe, waiting for me at the cabin when I arrive sometime past midnight. We will spend four or five days, talking and fishing, and reaffirming our reasons for being there, and being together. But Lagniappe, our cabin, and Jeru, our creek, cannot alone provide me the safe bridge to the future, nor the high ground on which to escape the uncertainty ahead. I know that I have to do that myself. I must find home in the present, not only in the memories of the reified past. And finding home in the now takes more courage, and creates more fear. The home I hunt is unknown, and forces me to think more consciously about what is important, not just what is comfortable or what is certain. So, the beautiful place where we now live, the woman whose life I share, the growth-producing challenges we face daily, the new friends we discover, and the Congregational church on Tejon and St. Vrain in Colorado Springs that affirms the search for justice and for kindness—these all portend the construction of a residence that will shelter. But I still cannot, nor do I wish for, escape from the truth that Jeru Creek and the cabin Lagniappe and the Pack River do give me an isolated retreat, a secluded place to rest a little, to recapture my grounding, to define my direction and, in my memories and in my aspirations, to come home to river earth.

About the Author

THE CHILD OF A DUSTBOWL- and depression-buffeted family, John Pierce was raised amidst hope and roots in the lowland forests and prairies of western Washington. Three decades of toil in universities on all edges of the country have never separated him from that earlier life. Pierce loves streams and rivers and their intermingled movement and stability. Life on that moving water has helped teach him who he is and why. His reflections on rivers have bound him tightly both to his past and to his future, and to the people around him.

John Pierce is author, co-author, or co-editor of more than a dozen scholarly books, and nearly a hundred journal articles and edited book chapters. President Bill Clinton appointed him a trustee of the Columbus Foundation, and Governor Mike Lowry appointed him to the board of the Washington Commission on the Humanities. He served as Dean of the College of Liberal Arts at Washington State University in Pullman, and now is Vice Chancellor of the University of Colorado at Colorado Springs, where he lives with his wife Ardith. But none of that prepared him for what he learned about himself when taking the previously untrod, humbling path of personal discovery mapped in this book of essays.